DISCARD

Goths

Recent Titles in
Guides to Subcultures and Countercultures

The Ku Klux Klan: A Guide to an American Subculture
Martin Gitlin

Hippies: A Guide to an American Subculture
Micah L. Issitt

Punks: A Guide to an American Subculture
Sharon M. Hannon

Beatniks: A Guide to an American Subculture
Alan Bisbort

Guides to
Subcultures and
Countercultures

Goths
A Guide to an American Subculture

Micah L. Issitt

GREENWOOD

AN IMPRINT OF ABC-CLIO, LLC
Santa Barbara, California • Denver, Colorado • Oxford, England

Publ.   1/13/12   93500

306.1
I 55

Library of Congress Cataloging-in-Publication Data

Issitt, Micah L.
  Goths : a guide to an American subculture / Micah L. Issitt.
    p. cm. — (Guides to subcultures and countercultures)
  Includes bibliographical references and index.
    ISBN 978–0–313–38604–6 (hbk. : alk. paper)—ISBN 978-0-313-38605-3 (ebook)
1. Goth culture (Subculture)—United States. I. Title.
HQ796.I78   2011
306'.10973—dc22   2010048010

ISBN: 978–0–313–38604–6
EISBN: 978–0–313–38605–3

15 14 13 12 11   1 2 3 4 5

This book is also available on the World Wide Web as an eBook.
Visit www.abc-clio.com for details.

Greenwood
An Imprint of ABC-CLIO, LLC

ABC-CLIO, LLC
130 Cremona Drive, P.O. Box 1911
Santa Barbara, California 93116-1911

*This book is dedicated to Carlyn and Jenna,
whom I love very much and whose help was
absolutely indispensable during the writing process, and
to all those out there who feel like freaks
and outcasts, you are not alone!*

Contents

Series Foreword   ix

Introduction   xi

Timeline   xvii

Chapter One   History of Goth   1

Chapter Two   Goth Music and the Dark Sound   17

Chapter Three   Fashion, Bodies, and Beauty   31

Chapter Four   Goth Fiction and Fantasy   47

Chapter Five   The Community of Goth   59

Chapter Six   The Perennial Gothic   69

Biographical Sketches   81

Glossary of Goth Slang   111

Primary Documents   115

Annotated Bibliography   147

Index   155

Series Foreword

From Beatniks to Flappers, Zoot Suiters to Punks, this series brings to
life some of the most compelling countercultures in American history.
Designed to offer a quick, in-depth examination and current perspective
on each group, the series aims to stimulate the reader's understanding
of the richness of the American experience. Each book explores a
countercultural group critical to American life and introduces the reader
to its historical setting and precedents, the ways in which it was
subversive or countercultural, and its significance and legacy in American
history. *Webster's Ninth New Collegiate Dictionary* defines counterculture
as "a culture with values and mores that run counter to those of
established society." Although some of the groups covered can be
described as primarily subcultural, they were targeted for inclusion
because they have not existed in a vacuum. They have advocated for
rules that methodically opposed mainstream culture, or lived by those
ideals to the degree that it became impossible not to impact the society
around them. They have left their marks, both positive and negative,
on the fabric of American culture. Volumes cover such groups as Hippies
and Beatniks, who impacted popular culture, literature, and art; the
Eco-Socialists and Radical Feminists, who worked toward social and

political change; and even groups such as the Ku Klux Klan, who left mostly scars.

A lively alternative to narrow historiography and scholarly monographs, the *Counterculture* series volumes can be described as a "library in a book," containing both essays and browsable reference materials, including primary documents, to enhance the research process and bring the content alive in a variety of ways. Written for students and general readers, each volume includes engaging illustrations, a timeline of critical events in the subculture, topical essays that illuminate aspects of the subculture, a glossary of subculture terms and slang, biographical sketches of the key players involved, and primary source excerpts—including speeches, writings, articles, first-person accounts, memoirs, diaries, government reports, and court decisions—that offer a contemporary perspective on each group. In addition, each volume includes an extensive bibliography of current recommended print and nonprint sources appropriate for further research.

Introduction

Gothic Guide

This book is an introductory guide to goth subculture in the United States and its sister groups around the world. As will be explored in these chapters, goth is a subculture with very deep roots, perhaps linked directly to the very foundations of the human psyche. The modern version of the subculture, which might just as well be called "goth rock" culture or "goth music" culture, has spread around the world, with major pockets in the United States, Europe, and Asia. While the modern subculture has its roots in 1980s England, it now has followers in areas as disparate as Japan and Argentina.

In its most basic sense, goth consists of a group of people who celebrate and indulge in darker elements of style, sound, and other aesthetic avenues. When the subculture peaked in the 1980s, it was focused on music, and "goth music" has remained one of the central elements of the culture. However, in the decades since goth came out of England, other aspects of the culture, including fashion and art, have become increasingly important threads binding members together into a community.

Goth has become well known in American media because of its association with teen violence, but, as will be explored later, the links between goth and violence are tenuous at best. Goth has also played a role in fostering a type of creative expression that has in turn become a more central part of modern American culture, and it has provided a sense of belonging for many who felt a lack of connection with mainstream modes of behavior.

As with any reference or introductory text, the aim here is to explore the most basic questions about the subculture, including "What is goth?" "How did goth culture come about?" and "What is the significance of goth in modern culture?"

The study of subcultures can be problematic for a number of reasons. First, members of subcultures tend to be wary of outside investigations and interpretations of their culture. Members of subcultures can be reluctant to talk openly about themselves. This may be primarily because subcultures are often misrepresented in mainstream accounts, especially in the pages of local and national news media. This has long been true of the relationship between media and subcultures. Hippies, for instance, were linked to rising divorce rates in the 1960s, largely by those who saw the hippies as a symbol of declining adherence to "American values." Similarly, goths have been lumped in with television and video games as potential culprits behind teenage violence.

Because subcultures are by definition different from the mainstream, and because this difference is often advertised in visual ways, many subcultures serve as convenient scapegoats for a variety of social ills. Members of subcultures have therefore come to distrust the mainstream press, feeling that they are never truly understood and that it is best to avoid contact with the press, or in fact any researcher attempting to investigate their culture.

While it is often difficult, the study of subcultures is also essential to our understanding of how society functions. The forces behind the emergence and decline of subcultures are primary agents of social evolution. It is often within fringe groups that aesthetic and social innovations first take hold, long before they become part of the mainstream.

This volume was developed using research from a variety of sources. Interviews with goths in both the United States and Europe form an important part of the basic foundation for this book, followed by investigations of the culture's own media, specifically the "fanzines" and other goth publications in print and in cyberspace. Finally, a significant amount of research for this volume was taken from scholarly works produced by literary researchers, sociologists, and other academic professionals who have conducted detailed, painstaking studies of the subculture and its history.

This book therefore functions both as an introduction for the general reader and as a basic sociological text. In the course of investigating goth history and the modern goth culture, this book will also provide information about how sociologists study subcultures in general. The primary aim here is to approach goth from a variety of angles, giving weight both to the goths' own descriptions of their culture and to the more objective views of the culture from without.

Subculture versus Counterculture

Sociologists make a distinction between a "subculture" and a "counterculture," though the two terms are generally used interchangeably outside of academic circles. A subculture can be generally defined as any distinct cultural group within a larger culture. A counterculture, by contrast, is a type of subculture characterized by the development of ideologies, aesthetics, or other beliefs that are in direct *opposition* to the larger culture.

Goth culture is an example of a subculture, rather than a counterculture. While the goths may hold beliefs and values that are considered "subversive" within the larger culture, goths are not focused on opposing mainstream culture, but rather on finding likeminded individuals with whom they can indulge in their alternative lifestyles within the larger framework of society.

This distinction is important because it speaks to the "goals" of the subculture. Whereas 1960s counterculturalists often fantasized about somehow being able to "destroy the system" and install a new and better system, members of subcultures generally celebrate being part of a smaller, more inclusive group that is outside of the mainstream. Whereas countercultures may want to replace the mainstream, a subculture has meaning and significance only insofar as there remains a mainstream for them to be different from.

Subcultures can form whenever a group becomes sufficiently distinct or cohesive to constitute a distinct culture within a culture. This can be fans of a certain type of music or a television program or a single book, or a more widespread phenomenon like police culture, Amish merchants, or people who use Twitter. In addition, subcultures are not mutually exclusive and a person can belong to more than one group within a culture. A dedicated Twitterer who also works for the police and goes to goth clubs on the weekend might indeed play an active role in all of these subcultures simultaneously.

The distinguishing factor is that the members of the subculture see themselves as "different" and "separate" from the mainstream in definitive ways. The subculture is a participatory culture, in which members choose to become part of the group. An ethnic group, for instance, is not automatically a subculture simply because members share an ethnicity that is different from the majority. However, if members of this ethnic group participate in cultural activities that set them apart, they may then constitute a distinct subculture.

This "participatory element" does not mean that members of the subculture need to accept (and they often do not) the labels used in the mainstream to define and distinguish their group. Many of those usually called "goths" vehemently deny that they are part of any such group, preferring to view themselves as unique individuals whose aesthetic choices are entirely their own. Others have chosen to embrace the idea that they are part of a distinct culture, whether they call it "goth," "dark culture," or simply "people like me."

If the values, beliefs, or aesthetics of a subculture become too popular, the subculture can be absorbed into the mainstream. This is, in fact, the natural end point in the life cycle of most subcultures. In the course of normal social evolution, mainstream society may come to embrace the ideologies, values, and aesthetics of its fringe groups. This is partially because subcultures and countercultures are sources of innovation, but also because members of subcultures age and join mainstream society, bringing elements of their subculture into their increasingly conventional lives. Sociologists sometimes refer to subcultures being "resorbed" or "assimilated," like so many Starfleet officers being "Borg-ed."

Goth culture provides an interesting example of a subculture in that it is both very long lived, in comparison to other aesthetic subcultures, and highly resistant to absorption and dilution. Goth has remained distinct and cohesive in situations where many other subcultures might have bled completely into the larger culture stream. In Germany, goth has even become an accepted part of mainstream music and fashion, without losing its distinctiveness or what some might call its "authenticity."

Finding Goths

Goths sometimes play a game called "spot the goth," in which a goth and his or her friends compete to catch sight of goths in public places, especially in places where one would not expect to see goths. On one hand, this is little more than a diversion for goths on a road trip, while on the other it indicates something very prominent in the subculture— a sense of kinship that often transcends traditional boundaries. Not all goths feel this sense of community and, in fact, some do not see themselves as part of a community or culture of any kind. Some goths, however, feel that they have more in common with goths from a different country than they may have with their own neighbors or even family.

While there are goths in many countries, this book will pay particular attention to goths in the United States, England, and Germany, three of the major epicenters of the subculture. Goths are most abundant in German cities like Leipzig, where "spot the goth" can be exhausting because of the frequency of encounters. Major American cities like New York, Philadelphia, and Los Angeles also have large goth scenes, but conduct most of their meetings in relative obscurity and through underground networks of friends. This volume will treat community as one of the most important aspects of goth culture and will attempt to address the ways in which community defines goth as the culture spreads.

Goth may seem alien to some, who see little appeal in the music, the fashion, or any other aspect of the culture. Some in the mainstream dismiss goths as a "mopey," "moody" bunch of kids, overly obsessed with death and other unsettling things. Goth culture is more, however, than the stereotypes commonly ascribed to it. Goth culture is creative, imaginative, and humorous, and it speaks to something that is very basic to human nature. To truly understand goth culture, we must first find that part of goth that is inside all of us, the ability to find beauty in the dark and disturbing. Goth may be defined by its difference from mainstream culture, but as the darker side of human nature is part of every person, goth can also be seen as a reflection of something that lies within the mainstream. Thus the primary focus of goth is not simply to be different from the mainstream, but rather to explore and even to celebrate those aspects of the human psyche that most try to deny, but that remain an essential part of the cultural substrate common to all cultures throughout time.

Timeline

238 AD	The Germanic goths invade a portion of the Roman Empire containing the modern Macedonia, Romania, and the Balkans.
1144	The Abbey of Saint Denis is completed and often cited as the first gothic structure.
1431–76	Vlad III (aka Vlad the Impaler), inspiration for Bram Stoker's fictional character "Count Dracula" and goth fashion icon, lives his life in Wallachia (now part of Romania).
1817	Mary Shelley releases one of the most famous gothic novels, *Frankenstein*.
1861	The Victorian Court of Mourning brings funerary attire into modern European fashion.
1897	Bram Stoker publishes *Dracula*, which becomes one of the most beloved gothic novels.
1965	The Doors form in Los Angeles. The band's dark, psychedelic sound is later seen as a precursor to the punk and goth musical movements.

1967	Journalist John Stickney, writing in *The Williams College News*, describes the Doors' music as "gothic rock."
	The Peel Sessions begin broadcasting and become an early venue for punk, new wave, goth, and ska bands in the United Kingdom.
1969	The Stooges form with front man Iggy Pop.
	David Bowie's second, self-titled album is released and becomes a major inspiration to the burgeoning new wave, goth, and futurist movements.
	UK music magazine *Zig Zag* publishes its first issue. The magazine supports the punk scene and later the goth scene.
1970	The Stooges release *Fun House*, later called one of the first punk rock albums.
1971	The New York Dolls form in New York City and become early proponents of the hard rock, glam rock, and pre-punk sound.
1973	The club CBGB opens in Manhattan in New York City, headed by musician Hilly Kristal.
	The Middle East oil crisis initiated by OPEC leads to recessions in the United Kingdom and the United States.
1974	The Ramones form in Queens, New York, and are later called one of the earliest pure punk rock bands.
1975	The Sex Pistols form in London under the management of Malcolm McLaren.
1976	Journalist Caroline Coon coins the term "Bromley Contingent" in *Melody Maker*.
	Siouxsie Sioux forms Siouxsie and the Banshees in London.

The Clash forms in London.

Joy Division forms in Manchester, UK.

Journalist Mick Mercer begins writing the fanzine *Panache*, later recognized as one of the first media sources to focus on goth music.

Anne Rice publishes *Interview with a Vampire*.

1977   John Keenan starts the F-Club in Leeds, UK, a moving "club night."

1978   Joy Division manager Anthony Wilson describes the band's music as "gothic" in a BBC Television interview.

An article in *New Music Express* labels Siouxsie and the Banshees as "gothic."

Factory Records, often considered the first goth label, opens in Manchester, UK.

June 14, 1979   Joy Division releases *Unknown Pleasures*, the first release for Factory Records.

September 15, 1979   Joy Division makes their only appearance on British television on the BBC2 show *Something Else*. Anthony Wilson describes the band's sound as "gothic" in an interview.

September 24, 1979   Bauhaus releases "Bela Lugosi's Dead."

UK Decay forms in Luton, UK.

1980   The Sisters of Mercy forms in Leeds, UK.

DJs Joseph Brooks and Henry Peck open Vinyl Fetish in La Brea, California, one of the first record stores in the United States to feature punk and goth music.

February 1981   In an article for the magazine *Sounds*, UK Decay front man Steven "Abbo" Abbot describes UK Decay as into the "gothic thing."

Joseph Brooks opens one of the first goth/punk clubs in the United States, The Veil, at Cathay de Grade, in Hollywood.

	Southern Death Cult forms in Bradford, Yorkshire, UK.
1982	Journalist Mick Mercer begins writing for *Zig Zag*, a music magazine, and soon becomes editor, steering the magazine toward dedicated coverage of goth music, fashion, and culture.
July 1982	The Batcave opens on Meard Street in London's SoHo district.
March 1983	Journalist Mick Mercer writes an article in *Melody Maker* that describes the new music as part of an emerging subculture scene.
	The Batcave, and DJ Hamish McDonald, go on a tour of England, helping to inspire the developing goth scenes around the country.
1986	The darkwave band Black Tape for a Blue Girl releases their debut album, *The Rope*.
1987	The goth rock club Slimelight opens in an abandoned church on High Holborn in London.
	Storm Constantine publishes *The Enchantments of Flesh and Spirit*.
1988	Entrepreneur Orv Madden opens the Hot Topic chain of boutiques.
	Tim Burton releases *Beetlejuice*.
1989	Neil Gaiman begins writing *The Sandman* comics.
1990	Tim Burton releases *Edward Scissorhands*.
November 1, 1991	Alt.gothic goes online.
1992	The first Wave-Gotik-Treffen festival is held in Leipzig, Germany.
	Poppy Z. Brite publishes *Lost Souls*.
1994	The Catwalk club opens in Seattle and becomes a central place for the Pacific Northwest goth and S&M scenes.

	Fear Cult forms in Los Angeles and releases the album *A Bouquet of Songs*.
	Faith and the Muse releases their debut album, *Elyria*.
1995	The first Convergence gathering is held in Chicago.
1996	Joseph Brooks creates Coven 13, a roving "goth night" venue that appears at clubs around Los Angeles, most notably the Mogus Club in Hollywood.
1997	Bellevue, Washington, teenagers are arrested for four murders. The assailants are described as involved in "goth culture."
April 1999	The Columbine High School massacre takes place. The assailants are later described as involved in a "goth lifestyle."
August 2000	*E!* Entertainment Television holds a goth fashion show.
	The first M'era Luna festival takes place in Hildesheim, Germany.
	Gothic Beauty magazine begins publication.
	New Grave magazine begins publication.
2004	Members of Convergence 9 in Las Vegas set out on the first annual goth cruise.
2008	The Japanese dark rock band Dir en Grey becomes one of the first visual kei bands to tour the United States.
2009	The documentary film *Goth Cruise* is released, documenting the annual goth cruise created by members of Convergence.
May 2010	Germany's largest dark music festival, Wave Gotik Treffen, takes play in Leipzig, attracting more than 25,000 attendees.

CHAPTER ONE

History of Goth

It is difficult to positively define goth subculture, and far easier to say that goth is NOT a cult, NOT a religion, and NOT a youth movement. At its roots, goth is a modern version of an aesthetic with very, very old roots. Derived from medieval conquest, fueled by dark romanticism, and reinvented in twentieth-century youth culture, the title has been transferred from generation to generation, taking on new meanings with each manifestation.

The original Goths (this is Goths with a capital "G") were a tribe of Germanic origin (largely from Sweden) that moved into the area that is now southern Russia in the second century AD. The Goths evolved from a scattered group of barbarian tribes into a massive kingdom that left its mark across Europe. The name "Goths" took on a meaning derived from these conquerors—a reference to destruction, mourning, and loss.[1]

The gothic label was later used by Renaissance critics to describe a type of art and architecture representative of the culture that (both literally and symbolically) destroyed the remnants of the Romanesque period. This new aesthetic was criticized as overly heavy, dark, and melancholy.[2] Then there was the "gothic literature" of the late 1700s and early 1800s, a style of fiction that blends elements of horror and

THE GOTHIC LANGUAGE

The Germanic Goths developed a language called the "Gothic language," which was similar to old high German and was used from the fourth to sixth centuries AD. Today it survives in historic religious texts. In their language, Goths might have referred to the modern subculture as a "kuni," or tribe.

romance to create lush fables of human nature, often (again, literally and symbolically) confronting forces of evil, darkness, and ignorance. One interesting facet of the genre was the blurring of lines between good and evil, with villainous heroes and sympathetic monsters in stories that evoke raw human passions.[3]

What do Gothic tribes, medieval cathedrals, and romantic novels have to do with the twenty-first-century subculture that has come to wear this medieval mantle? The word "goth" has been used again and again to describe vastly different aspects of human culture related by their association to a similar look, sound, or feel—a touch of the dark and melancholy, a hint of horror tinged with romance. These are the threads that tie the modern goth to the vaunted arches of a Gothic cathedral.

As of this writing, goths are not planning a European takeover, nor are they (with possible exceptions) designing many cathedrals; they are the stewards of an underground aesthetic that has been part of human culture ever since the first humans saw something beautiful in the midst of something horrifying. Unlike previous incarnations, however, *this* goth is born from music.

Dark Rock to Punk

Leaping ahead from the 1770s to the 1970s, the roots of the new goth become clearer. Music historians nearly universally agree that goth music came out of the post-punk mélange of the early 1980s, but its roots go back further, to the darker tones of 1960s psychedelia.

Psychedelic rock began on an upbeat note, but by the late 1960s bands like The Velvet Underground and The Doors began exploring darker sonic concoctions and moody melodies, with lyrics that high-lighted the shadier elements of humanity. The Velvet Underground's Lou Reed wrote songs about drug addiction and insanity, while most rock bands of the same era were writing songs that were considerably lighter in tone. The Doors may have been the first band to be labeled "gothic rock," as they were described by reviewer John Stickney in a 1967 review for *The Williams College News.*[4]

Experimental bands—those whose sound transcends contempo-rary genres—often emerge from major musical centers, where there are a lot of musicians vying for time at center stage. In the 1970s United Kingdom, London was this kind of scene, with a plethora of new bands emerging all the time, pushing the limits of every genre. South London native David Bowie was one of those experimental artists whose music was so innovative that it required a new musical language. In the early 1970s, he created "glam rock."

Bowie appears on the inspiration lists of hundreds of artists spanning many genres. While goth music proper would not emerge for some years, Bowie already embodied some of the qualities that would later fall into the overall goth aesthetic: he favored an androgynous appearance, his lyrics were at times moody and introspective, and there was more than a little theater to his version of rock.[5]

Bowie and his glam rock inspired most of those who would go on to make "goth music," but they had other influences as well. As sixties rock emerged partially in rebellion to the culturally repressive environment of the 1950s, so the 1960s had its own backlash, sweeping across many aspects of culture. Part of this backlash was an intense dissatisfaction with the mainstream and a growing sense that popular music, literature, and culture itself was in a state of stagnation. The atmosphere was primed for an explosion, and then, from the garages of the United States and Britain, punk rock hit the scene.

Punk Runs into the Post

Punk rock cannot really be traced to either the United States or the United Kingdom. Rather, the scene emerged on two different fronts, both answering the same call. Some of the most influential pre-punk bands were American in origin. From Ann Arbor, Michigan, came

Iggy Pop and the Stooges, an energetic rock band whose first two albums, *The Stooges* (1969) and *Funhouse* (1970), had a powerful influence on the evolving punk sound.[6] Similarly, the New York Dolls, from New York City, began performing in 1971 and were the inspiration for many of the British punk bands that formed in subsequent years.[7]

Punk did not emerge in a vacuum; a variety of elements were converging to make it possible for this new genre to spread in dramatic fashion. Some music historians have suggested that widespread recessions, some related to the OPEC oil crisis of the 1970s, helped to create the environment for the emergence of punk, with massive unemployment fueling a growing dissatisfaction among the populace.[8]

Second, the 1960s left both the United States and the United Kingdom with a small army of alternative music and cultural publications reporting on bands that were outside the mainstream. It was these magazines, like Britain's *Zig Zag* (started in 1969), that gave this new genre its name. In later years, these same magazines would help to popularize the "post-punk" genres, including early goth music.

Underground and alternative radio programs also played a major role in popularizing new sounds. In Britain, John Ravenscroft, better known as John Peel, started broadcasting a series of radio programs in 1968 that would become one of the first and best venues for emerging artists. Over the years, his Peel Sessions broadcasts featured a veritable who's who of punk, new wave, and goth bands that later gained international fame.

In 1971, musician and art school student Malcolm McLaren started a little shop in London's Chelsea district selling music, clothing, and other goods. McLaren's Too Fast to Live, Too Young to Die was one of the first shops of its kind to cater to the underground sound *and* the underground look. As punk came along, McLaren sold the accompanying records and other wares.[9] In 1972, after a trip to New York, McLaren became manager for the New York Dolls and helped to bring the band's new sound across the ocean.

Then came the Sex Pistols. Formed in 1975, with McLaren as their manager, the Sex Pistols became the biggest band in the London punk scene.[10] While McLaren hoped his new find would emulate the sound of The Ramones, one of the most popular bands from the U.S. punk scene, the Sex Pistols had different ideas, creating their own,

POST-PUNK GENRES

England's post-punk musical period bequeathed goth, new wave, and other genres to the world. The genre known as "art rock," a blend of rock music with performance art, came out of this era, as did "British ska," a style that blends reggae with pop and new wave.

uniquely British take on the punk theme that would eventually stand as the template for punk rock as a whole.

By 1976, Sex Pistols concerts had become the most important social events of the musical underground. With a cadre of fans following from venue to venue, loving punk music became a subculture unto itself. Journalist Caroline Coon, writing in *Melody Maker* magazine, coined the moniker "Bromley Contingent" for one group of fans that formed the core of the Sex Pistols audience, many of whom hailed from the town of Bromley.[11] Members of this group and other Sex Pistols fans, inspired to take on music themselves, later became the originators of the family of styles that came to be called "post-punk," which included genres like "new wave" and "goth."

The Birth of Proto-Goth

Punk rock has often been described as a DIY genre, in which clothing, instrumentation, production, and everything else was second to the raw energy of the music. The post-punk bands took things in a different direction, creating outrageous fashions that blended elements of the punk, postapocalyptic look with the glamour of David Bowie and the glam rock stars.

Post-punk music headed in many different directions at once. On one hand, some bands followed a pop-driven route, later falling under the rubric "new wave." On the other, there were a number of bands doing something a bit darker and more theatrical. This new genre was initially called "positive punk," because of their more positive and atmospheric sound. Among them was Siouxsie and the Banshees, which formed in 1976 and hailed the coming of goth, in both sound and fashion. Lead singer Siouxsie Sioux adopted what became a characteristic dark goth look, while her music fell into the middle ground between punk that what would later be called "goth."[12]

Also in 1976, Joy Division formed, again by people who were part of the dedicated Sex Pistols following. Joy Division and lead singer Ian Curtis were unique in their time, but became a major influence on future goth musicians. It was Joy Division's manager Anthony Wilson who first described the band's sound as "gothic" in a 1978 interview for the BBC. That same year, an article in *New Music Express* used the same term to describe Siouxsie and the Banshees.[13]

The following year, Luton-based band UK Decay and the London-based Bauhaus began releasing music, later recognized as two of the most important early goth bands. The Bauhaus single "Bela Lugosi's Dead" became a goth anthem in the decade to come, and inspired many of the musicians who would go on to form the next generation of goth.[14]

In 1978, business partners Anthony Wilson, Martin Hannett, Peter Saville, and Alan Erasmus opened The Factory Club on Royce Road in Manchester, UK, and founded Factory Records, which became the first label to cater to the emerging goth genre. Factory's first releases included the Bauhaus album *Unknown Pleasures*, released in 1979.

Graphic artist Peter Saville designed the cover for the first Bauhaus album, choosing a plain black background with a white image of sonic topography as the sole graphic. The resulting cover (now iconic in the genre) was eye-catching and unique and became the standard "look" for the goth album over the next decade. In fact, Factory Records' style of promotion and marketing set the tone for the entire goth industry over the next decade.

Links between this new sound and the other phenomena to bear the "gothic" title were not coincidental. From a musical perspective, these new bands used effects to create atmosphere. Heavy, slow, repetitive drums and guitars filtered thorough deep echoes combined to create a sound that was eerie and hazy, yet captivating. The lyricists of this new field wrote about unfulfilled romance and isolation, using "somber, metaphorical vocals."[15] As far as fashion was concerned, the new uniform was stark, black, and focused on contrast and shadow.

Similar adjectives were and are used to describe romantic gothic literature and architecture. Those who gave the genre its name were drawing on historical reflections and creating links between this new music and an undercurrent aesthetic hundreds of years old. This was a modern "gothic" thing, a new take on a very old idea.

Goth's First Wave

The new bands required new media, and a variety of magazines and venues began focusing their attention on these post-punk outfits. In 1981, DJ Joseph Brooks opened The Veil in La Brea, California, one of the first venues to feature goth music in the United States. The following year, journalist Mick Mercer, publisher of a small but influential British "fanzine" called *Panache* (started in 1976), became editor of England's *Zig Zag* magazine. Over the next decade, Mercer's coverage helped to put the early goth bands in the spotlight.

Also in 1982, the now famous Batcave club opened on Meard Street in London. The Batcave was the most famous goth club, hosting all the early goth bands and a host of newcomers and startups. The Batcave was also important from a community perspective, helping fans of this new music to congregate and creating avenues for distribution of music, news, fashion, and everything else that appealed to this contingent of the post-punk environment.[16] In 1983, the Batcave club started a touring "goth night," which moved around the country appearing in various clubs and leaving newly anointed goth fans in its wake. Another London club, Slimelight, which opened in 1987, carried on the Batcave torch, becoming a focal place for goths and goth music.

It was during this time, from the early to mid-1980s, that a recognizable subculture developed around the music scene. These fans came together because of their interest in the new music, but soon found that they had other interests in common—a similar sense of fashion and complementary interests in movies, books, and other media. In a 1983 article from *Zig Zag*, writer Tom Vague referred to the fans, rather than just the music, as "goth" and the label stuck, spreading throughout the media and becoming the tag for a culture, rather than simply a genre.[17]

At the same time, the goth scene in the United States was developing. The band Christian Death, which started in 1979, was

Members of the British punk band The Clash are shown, 1983. From left: Joe Strummer, Mick Jones, Terry Chimes, and Paul Simonon. (AP Photo)

one of the most important anchors for the Los Angeles scene, and also a precursor for a new subgenre—an amped-up, more aggressive take on the gothic theme that was later called "deathrock."[18]

It was around 1989 that Projekt Records, a New York–based independent label, started releasing collections from unknown new bands, representing goth and other subgenres developing under that umbrella. Over the course of the 1990s, Projekt would become one of the premier American labels for music in the goth family.[19]

Goth reached such popularity that it began to transition from the underground to the mainstream. The clothing chain Hot Topic started in 1988 and appeared in shopping malls across the world, featuring, among other items, goth-inspired clothing and music mixes.[20] To some, clothing stores like Hot Topic and similar "popularized" variations on the theme represented the end of a "golden age," when a phenomenon that had once been more or less exclusive to people "in the know" became too popular. Now, in addition to those with some credibility in the scene, there were "mall goths" and "teeny bopper goths," who imitated the style and listened to the music, but were often perceived as outsiders.

The Second Wave

Many music historians and researchers have identified the early to mid-1980s as the "first wave" of the goth subculture, when the music and the culture were largely centered in England, with some stirrings in the United States. In the late 1980s and early 1990s, goth had what some have called a "second wave," which led from the traditional goth music and style to a whole plethora of subgenres around the world.[21]

The U.S. scene largely developed during the so-called second wave. For one thing, goth music proper inspired new developments in rock and metal that blurred the lines between the genres and brought the dark sound to a wider audience. Trent Reznor and his band Nine Inch Nails, a blend of rock and industrial music sometimes called "industrial metal," became a phenomenon in the early 1990s. Some fans of more traditional goth music also enjoyed Reznor's unique goth fusion, and Nine Inch Nails appealed to a larger, more pop-oriented crowd. Those attracted to this new dark rock sometimes developed interest in more traditional goth bands as well, increasing the popularity of the genre as a whole.

The early 1990s largely saw the end of dedicated goth clubs, and in their place, a proliferation of "goth nights" emerged around the United Kingdom and the United States. Goth nights generally started as the project of one or a couple of DJs who spun a variety of traditional goth and new genres, including goth-infused dance music like EBM (electro body movement) and darkwave, and traveled from club to club, appearing once or twice a month.

These goth nights became gathering points for local networks, centered around a city or, in larger cities, around a certain neighborhood.[22] While goth music spawned subgenres, the subculture itself also splintered into different groups with different musical interests, fashion choices, and other tastes. Goth fashion produced subgroups like "cybergoths," "vampire goths," and "Gothic Lolitas." Goth style shared certain elements with the fetish/S&M scene from the days when Siouxsie Sioux inspired a generation of women with her sexualized apparel. In the 1990s, elements of fetish style became more common in some parts of the goth scene, especially in the United States.

A FAMILY OF DARK GENRES

In addition to traditional goth rock, a number of dark music genres have become associated with goth culture, including:

deathrock
medieval rock
neo folk
EBM
darkwave
synthpop
electropop
gothabilly
cold wave
industrial metal
electro industrial
cyber metal
emo

In the United States and England, the general trend among the older goth community was to take their culture underground, while goth-inspired pop music and fashion went mainstream. For the next 20 years, the U.S. goth scene remained largely underground, while in other countries, especially Germany, goth hit the mainstream like never before. The German goth scene was the largest in the world by the late 1990s, and spawned its own subgenres, including "middle-ages goth" and "neo folk." German goth magazines were big enough to be sold on the major newsstands, rather than through specialty vendors, and similarly goth music from the different subgenres was distributed through mainstream music outlets.

Another major development in the 1990s was the emergence of goth cyberculture, largely initiated by the start of the alt.gothic newsgroup in November of 1991.[23] The newsgroup started humbly, with a few posters discussing music and the general goth lifestyle, and it quickly ballooned with hundreds of contributors eager to share their own opinions.

Journalist Mick Mercer, who made a career writing books and articles about goth music and culture, was a frequent contributor in the early days of alt.gothic, defending the culture and music against mainstream misconceptions and promoting the community element. Other newsgroups soon followed, the largest of which was uk.people .gothic, a site that became the major hub for British goths, while alt.gothic remained the primary site for American goths.

The community element of the subculture became stronger in the 1990s, fueled by the international spread of goth music and fashion, the development of new, localized scenes, and the proliferation of Internet communication. This started a new trend: goth festivals and gatherings.

Whitby Gothic Weekend has been held twice a year since 1995 in Whitby, England, a town that plays a role in Bram Stoker's famous vampire novel *Dracula*. Whitby attracts close to 2,000 gatherers each year, mainly from Britain, but some from the United States, Germany, Asia, and elsewhere. Other events, like Dracula's Ball in Philadelphia and M'era Luna in Germany, attract thousands of goths from both neighboring and extended communities. The festivals created links between goths from different areas, allowing for the exchange of music and fashion, and the promotion of other goth events to a wide audience. Through the Internet and the festivals, goth truly became a transnational culture linked through music and fashion across cultural and national boundaries.

Goth Defends Itself

In 1997, Alex Baranyi and David Anderson, two teenagers from the affluent Seattle suburb of Bellevue, were arrested in connection with the brutal murder of two teenage girls and their parents. The two assailants stabbed and beat their victims to death allegedly over minor issues, including the girls' refusal to share cigarettes and an outstanding debt of just over $300.

Interviews and police investigations revealed that the two friends had connections to what the media described as a "goth" style. Baranyi and Anderson wore dark clothing, whitened their faces with makeup, and listened to music characterized as "goth" and "dark metal." The Bellevue murders helped to spark a national debate about violence among teenagers, and some began suggesting that the teenagers' "goth" affiliations might have played a role in their becoming violent.[24]

In 1999, high school students Dylan Klebold and Eric Harris entered their high school armed with assault rifles and began opening fire on students and teachers, killing 13 people before committing suicide in the school's library. The story soon became worldwide news, and the debate over rising teenage violence intensified. Again friends and teachers identified Klebold and Harris as "goths," and media attacks against the music and the subculture escalated.[25]

Those with interest in defending the subculture debated the issue through the newsgroups, and the media interviewed many musicians and self-proclaimed members of the national goth community. Some claimed that the killers were not goth, while others took a more moderate stance, saying that Klebold and Harris's involvement in elements of the subculture was irrelevant because the vast majority of goths are not and have never been violent. The general message was that the Columbine shooters were simply troubled teens who happened to like things that were goth, rather than kids turned into killers through their association with goth music or imagery.[26]

The post-Columbine antigoth media campaign had lasting effects on the public consciousness. As the public searched for a way to understand the perceived rise in teenage violence, many in the media found goths a convenient scapegoat to explain the troubling trends. For some in mainstream America, this is the view of goth culture that would remain: a "cultlike" culture that glamorizes and even promotes violence through its music and its general focus on horror and disturbing imagery. For some in the goth community, the intense scrutiny brought about in the media strengthened ties, creating a sense of resistance to the ignorance and prejudice of the mainstream.

With the onset of the U.S. panic over terrorism following the September 2001 attack on the World Trade Center, goth paranoia was largely relegated to the back of the newspapers and goths once again resumed their normal activities without the same level of public scrutiny. The late 1990s are still regarded as a pivotal time for the subculture, introducing a public view of the culture that would persist throughout the first decade of the twenty-first century.

GOTH TO A 15-YEAR-OLD

Fifteen-year-old Kathryn Garnier (who goes by Kat McBride) is not a goth. A self-proclaimed "geek," she has grown up with goths as a familiar part of her environment. Kathryn created the following list of "things that goths like":

    writing dark poetry
    clove cigarettes
    going to clubs
    art
    makeup

Goth in the New Millennium

While many subcultures emerge and decline in a few short years, the goth phenomenon has evinced a tendency to survive, moving from the underground closer to the mainstream and back again. The reasons for this are myriad, including a persistent and very influential commercial aspect, an effective network of music distribution, dedicated online participation, and continued self-recruitment due to the culture's appeal to young adults and teenagers living in environments similar to those that first gave birth to goth music and fashion.

While it may be appropriate to say that goth has survived, the goth culture of 2010 bears little resemblance to its 1980 incarnations. It is not uncommon for elder goths to express the sentiment that goth has in fact died and been replaced by something else (generally something that they do not much care for). Depending on who you ask, you may learn that the goth scene is either dead and buried or alive and constantly evolving. The truth is, as always, in the eye of the goth (or nongoth).

Many goths loathe the goth label, perhaps because, for many, the quintessential goth quality is their inability to be labeled or described in a definite way. Those attracted to the subculture also tend to share a similar disdain for the way the mainstream culture categorizes, reduces, and minimizes those who are different. Still, the central tenet of goth culture is, and has always been, a reverence for those phenomena considered frightening or unsettling by most people.

These darker themes continue to exert a poignant, dramatic, and evocative influence, especially in contrast to the banality of day-to-day existence.

The aesthetic that inspired early goth music is still very much prevalent in global culture. The allure and mystery of the dark and the attraction of the atmospheric are still playing a role in the development of music, fashion, and other aspects of culture. It is perhaps this more widespread aesthetic potential that prevents goth from dying and continues to bring something dark to bear in our collective creativity and universal need for expression.

Notes

1. Peter Heather, *The Goths* (Hoboken, NJ: Wiley-Blackwell, 1998), 1–20.
2. Paul Frankl et al., *Gothic Architecture* (New Haven, CT: Yale University Press, 2000), 1–13.
3. David Punter and Glennis Byron, *The Gothic* (Hoboken, NJ: Wiley-Blackwell, 2004), 13–15.
4. Pete Scathe, "An Early History of Goth," 2010, http://www.scathe.demon.co.uk/name.htm (November 2010).
5. David Buckley, *David Bowie: A Complete Guide to His Music* (London: Omnibus Press, 2005), 3–30.
6. Stephen Colegrave and Chris Sullivan, *Punk: The Definitive Record of a Revolution* (New York: Thunder's Mouth Press, 2005), 45–50.
7. Ibid., 59–62.
8. Nabeel Zuberi, *Sounds English: Transnational Popular Music* (Champaign: University of Illinois Press, 2001), 68–72.
9. Max Wooldridge and Malcolm McLaren, *Rock 'N' Roll London* (New York: Macmillan, 2002), 43–46.
10. Lauraine Leblanc, *Pretty in Punk: Girls' Gender Resistance in a Boys' Subculture* (New Brunswick, NJ: Rutgers University Press, 1999), 37–40.
11. Karen Kelly and Evelyn McDonnell, *Stars Don't Stand Still in the Sky: Music and Myth* (New York: New York University Press, 1999), 80–85.
12. Ibid., 82–83.
13. Michael Bibby, "Atrocity Exhibitions: Joy Division, Factory Records, and Goth," in *Goth: Undead Subculture*, ed. Lauren M. Goodlad and Michael Bibby, 239 (Durham, NC: Duke University Press).
14. Ibid., 164.
15. Paul Hodkinson, *Goth: Identity, Style and Subculture* (New York: Berg, 2002), 47.
16. Lauren M. Goodland and Michael Bibby, "Introduction," in Goodlad and Bibby, *Goth*, 2.

17. Pete Scathe, "An Early History of Goth."
18. Dave Thompson, *Alternative Rock* (Milwaukee, WI: Mel Bay, 2000), 66–67.
19. Interview with Sam Rosenthal, March 9, 2010.
20. Joseph A. Kotarba and Phillip Vannini, *Understanding Society through Popular Music* (New York: Taylor & Francis, 2008), 65.
21. Carol Siegal, *Goth's Dark Empire* (Bloomington: Indiana University Press, 2005), 31–32.
22. Dunja Brill, *Goth Culture: Gender, Sexuality and Style* (New York: Berg, 2008), 3–4.
23. Tom Fosdyke, "Alt.gothic FAQ Version 3.2," http://www.faqs.org/faqs/alt-gothic-faq/ (accessed March 26, 2010).
24. Zafar Y. Ibrahim, *Shared Psychosis* (Lakewood, WA: Crispus Medical Press, 2003), 26–30.
25. Nancy Kilpatrick, *The Goth Bible: A Compendium for the Darkly Inclined* (New York: St. Martin's Griffin, 2004), 24–26.
26. Goodlad and Bibby, "Introduction," 12.

CHAPTER TWO

Goth Music and the Dark Sound

There is nothing more essential to goth culture than music. In the early days of goth, the music was the nucleus around which the culture first formed, and in the years since, musical preference has divided and subdivided the culture into cliques. In modern gothdom, fashion and the general aesthetic may be equally important to the evolution of the subculture, but the music is arguably still the central facet. Concerts and DJ goth nights remain the most ubiquitous gathering point for goths around the world, as sharing, comparing, and critiquing music is, for many, the bread and butter of being goth.

Goth music has mutated and diversified to such a degree since its inception that many of its subgenres and quirky sideline bands are only marginally connected to the aesthetic that bound the original goth bands into something resembling a cohesive musical movement. Modern goth music ranges from sparse, stripped-down pop to energetic electronica and hard-edged rock. Newer genres are sometimes rejected by elder goths, like misbehaving children disowned by their parents, but they still must be considered part of the overall scene. All of these now quite displaced subgenres are modern manifestations of a similar musical attitude that set the early goth bands apart in the post-punk landscape.

In *Goth: Identity, Style and Subculture*, researcher Paul Hodkinson states that knowledge of goth music, both past and present, is one of the most important ways that members of the subculture gain "capital," or status within the subculture.[1] Thus, from a sociological standpoint, the music is again a defining factor of the culture, and the exchange of music and musical knowledge one of the culture's most important conventions.

Defining Goth Music

Music is notoriously difficult to describe without resorting to dry jargon or technical descriptions of how musicians use their instruments to produce certain sounds. Technical terminology can help to classify and evaluate, but does little to communicate the experiential aspect.[2] In an effort to capture this more ineffable quality, critics use lists of adjectives to characterize the emotional impact and other aesthetic aspects of the sound. These efforts also inevitably fall short, because music appreciation is both highly personal and largely dependent on context and environment.

Music is rarely experienced simply as sound, but is accompanied by one or more associated bits of information. Album covers, posters, photos of band members, as well as the environment in which one first encounters a song or band, color the impression of the music and help listeners to associate the sound of one band with another, giving rise to genres.[3] Still, among fans, there is always disagreement about which bands belong within each genre and subgenre.

Most of the musicians interviewed for this volume were emphatic that their music was not "goth," and expressed dismay at the media's unfortunate tendency to pigeonhole their art with this maligned label.[4] Musicians tend to avoid conventional descriptions of genre when describing their own music and instead evoke a list of adjectives relating to the general feeling, emotional intent, or energy level of their sound. While few are willing to say, "My music is goth," their adjective lists tend to overlap and terms like "intense," "moody," "emotional," "atmospheric," and "dark" are frequently used to describe this antigeneric sound that the public labels "goth."[5]

Goth music is never distant from visual representations of the cultural style and associated interests. Album artwork and other band-related imagery provide fans with a clear message: this is how this music looks. Whitened faces and dark features, skulls, bats, coffins, vampires, crosses, arcane symbols, and other elements ripped from history were integral to the genre's "image" from the start. From there, both the accepted look and the accepted sound have expanded, while remaining tied to this basic look and feel.

There is no "goth sound" per se in 2010, but rather a group of bands that to some extent fall under an umbrella (a black umbrella, of course) woven from a set of descriptors like "poetic," "romantic," "bleak," and "distant." The modern scene contains bands that are far more energetic than their precursors, blending the "dark" sound with the driving energy of electronic dance music. Other bands have combined poetic, descriptive lyricism, a hallmark of the early goth sound, with elements of industrial and/or heavy metal instrumentation.

There are millions of possible combinations using at least some part of the basic formula. Fans around the world have a network of music importers at their disposal and can find not only "mainstream" bands that have cracked into radio play but also lesser known bands and compilation albums from around the world. Some older goths say that "goth is dead" and that the goth music that once existed is largely a thing of the past. However, for the young goths, who are only now donning their first ripped fishnets, this point in history represents the beginning of what may later be seen as goth's next wave.

The Traditional Goth Sound

The biographies of punk and goth icons overlap in one key area: during their childhoods and teenage years, these future artists often describe feeling a certain malaise, depression, and even anger focused on the banal environment of their lower- and middle-class white environments. This sense of isolation and dissatisfaction is generally seen as part of the driving force that led these youngsters to become poets, writers, and musicians.[6]

This is not to say that punk and goth music must always be sad or angry; at times bands in both genres express joy, humor, and optimism, though more often the music explores darker themes. Sadness, melancholy, and the general sense that life is painful and unfair have always played an important role in inspiring artists. In fact, the goth tendency to focus on the bitter reality of darker situations connects their music to the romantic literature of previous eras, when many poets and novelists also wrote about loss, loneliness, and isolation.[7]

The initial goth bands, like Siouxsie and the Banshees, Bauhaus, and Joy Division, coexisted with punk music, constituting an alternative to the anger-fueled punk sound. The goth sound was more cerebral, melodic and understated. The guitars were still there, but were placed in the back of the mix, propping up the melody rather than grinding out fuzzy rhythmic notes. Bass and synthesized sounds came to the forefront, providing both melodic lines and droning, rhythmic structures.[8]

Another major difference between goth and punk music is the general approach to lyricism. While the punks were literally yelling and screaming, the goths favored a more melodic and subdued tact. It was as if the punks were exploring their rage at the realization that life is painful and often meaningless, while the goths responded with resignation, outlining the reasons why life is painful and quietly explaining how they felt about it.[9]

The traditional goth sound was also informed by artists like David Bowie, who had a flair for costume and theatrics. Singer Siouxsie Sioux, arguably the first goth maven, used a variety of costumes and theatrical elements in crafting her stage persona. In many ways, spectacle was as important to the early goth thing as the music. Siouxsie Sioux's first performance, for instance, consisted of Siouxsie reciting the Lord's Prayer while her accompanying musicians experimented in the background.[10]

The early goth bands in America were very close in both fashion and overall sound to certain British new wave bands. Bands like The Cure, and lead singer Robert Smith, occupy a place between the happier side of new wave, like Flock of Seagulls, and the darker tones of Joy Division and the true goth bands. The two genres differed by degree and general attitude, with new wave bands choosing a slightly more upbeat and optimistic tone, but both genres emerged from the post-punk stew and overlapped in many ways.[11]

In modern terms, the original goth sound, especially Bauhaus, Joy Division, and Siouxsie and the Banshees, are lumped into a historical

GLITTER AND GLAM

Blending vintage Hollywood with splashes of science fiction and cabaret, glam rock, or "glitter rock," was popular in the early 1970s, but its effects reverberate into the twenty-first century. At its height the genre had dozens of bands in the United States and the United Kingdom, including T-Rex and Roxy Music.

category: eighties music. Joy Division songs are now played alongside The Cure and the lighter strains of eighties pop at new wave and "eighties nights" around the world, where they appeal to both new listeners and nostalgic 40- and 50-years-olds who may still own the original albums on vinyl.

Other members of the initial goth wave, bands like Sisters of Mercy and Christian Death, led the music in a slightly different direction. Their more aggressive take on the goth sound would eventually inspire the development of new subgenres, including gothic rock and death rock, and it played an important role in the scene over the ensuing decade.

American Gothic

Many of the pioneering goth bands were British, and the impetus of the culture was focused on the United Kingdom throughout the early and mid-1980s. American early goth bands, like Christian Death and 45 Grave, helped to make Los Angeles and the West Coast in general the focal point for the U.S. scene. Music imported from England inspired the new generation of bands, and the imported goth scene thrived.[12]

The U.S. goth scene of the 1980s and 1990s is a bit of a mess in terms of who was doing what, when. Bands like Black Tape for a Blue Girl, Christian Death, and Fear Cult emerged in the late 1980s, and played a role in developing the American goth environment. By the mid-1990s, a new subgenre, sometimes called "death rock" and sometimes "goth rock," emerged, largely led by Christian Death and bands that followed their example. Lead singer Rozz Williams also formed Shadow Project, after the breakup of Christian Death, a band that further developed the harder goth rock sound.[13]

Gothic rock retains melodic elements of the earlier goth sound, but the music is heavier, overlapping with metal and hard rock. Guitars and bass are used to create driving rhythms and the vocals are more primal and energetic. Elements of horror and themes that include ghostly sounds and the undead are also often woven into the goth rock or death rock sound. The genre was largely of U.S. origin, though bands in other countries developed similar styles.[14]

The death rock phenomenon influenced musicians like Marilyn Manson and Nine Inch Nails, whose music was sometimes placed under the heading "industrial metal" or "Nu Metal."[15] While these were never considered goth bands, the styles overlapped to some degree and many goths listened to industrial metal artists as well as goth proper.[16]

U.S. rock star Marilyn Manson performs at the Hallenstadion in Zurich, Switzerland, February 8, 2001. (AP Photo/Franco Greco)

By the late 1990s, the U.S. scene had produced a host of highly creative and unusual goth rock bands.[17] London After Midnight, a Los Angeles–based band often classified as "goth rock" and headed by Sean Brennan, is often cited as one of the most influential voices of the late 1990s goth scene, though Brennan (like many musicians considered part of the genre) vociferously denounces his connection to "goth music."[18]

A few of the American goth bands that emerged in the late 1980s and early 1990s continued into the twenty-first century, including Black Tape for a Blue Girl and Faith and the Muse. As the pioneering American goths aged, these early bands continued to add new innovation to the genre and inspire newer bands, effectively serving as leaders of a leaderless community.

European Expansion

Electronica, or "electronic dance music," is an offshoot of eighties experimental music aimed at dance clubs. Electronica includes a variety of genres, from those close to the disco sounds of the 1970s to those that are closer to hip-hop and rap music, with an urban, jazz-infused flavor. Goth and electronica began to blend in the 1990s, leading to a form of music called EBM or "electro body movement."[19]

While the United States led the way in goth rock, the 1990s saw the center of global goth culture shift from the United Kingdom to Germany. By the end of the decade, Germany boasted the world's largest goth community, with hundreds of bands and dozens of magazines, both mainstream and underground, covering the gothic music scene and its sister genres.[20]

THE GERMAN POWER STATION

Modern electronica was pioneered by the German band Kraftwerk, who produced instrumental, entirely computerized music in the 1970s and 1980s. A generation of DJs was inspired to take up the torch, later blending this computerized sound with disco to create the droning rhythms popular in dance clubs around the world.

The goth scene also flourished in Belgium, where the Belgians' fondness for both club music and goth proper inspired inroads between the two. Belgian and German DJs started the EBM genre by blending eighties goth and new wave with dance beats, and, from there, a few of these DJs began creating and selling original mixes of this darkly danceable potpourri. Though it emerged in Belgian and German clubs, EBM soon spread around Europe and overseas, becoming popular in U.S. nightclubs by the late 1990s.[21]

Music from the 1980s has long been a mainstay at dance clubs catering to white, middle-class audiences. The blend of eighties goth and dance music therefore capitalizes on this popularity and has proved an excellent way to inspire nostalgia-fueled dance mania in older clubgoers. In the twenty-first century, the United States saw a resurgence of interest in all things 1980s, from music to hairstyles. Though the new eighties craze appealed primarily to those who did most of their growing up in the nineties, the resurgence increased interest in EBM among younger audiences.

EBM and other types of "electro" music became hugely popular in Germany and, in 2010, constituted a dominant element of the national goth scene. The inventive Teutonic goths also developed styles that were uniquely German, including blending goth with one of their other highly original genres, "neo-medieval music."

Beginning in the late 1970s, a small musical movement in Germany saw the revival of secular medieval music and instrumentation, with artists playing lutes, medieval guitars, flutes, and a variety of other historical instruments alongside modern instruments to create a new kind of "medieval rock." This new music required a new costume, and the revival of medieval bard attire followed soon after. Goth culture had long had an affinity for the romantic appeal of dead generations, dead styles, and dead things in general, and so goth rock and medieval rock seemed destined to meet.

Since the 1990s, the German goths have embraced a handful of bands blending goth with medieval elements. Saltorio Mortis (Latin for "dance of death") produced dark medieval metal, while another popular band, Helium Vola, blended medieval and electronic music to create a sort of EBM medieval sound. The neo-medieval goth thing remained a small, fairly specialist genre, but quite popular with German goths.[22]

Another specialized subgenre created by bands in both Germany and the United Kingdom is the "neo-folk" style, a unique blend of historical sounds from various places in German and European history, with dark rock and electronic elements. The most popular modern proponents of the style largely hail from England, like Sol Invictus and Death in June, but most fans of the style are German.[23]

A somewhat more heavy metal–oriented type of goth music became popular in the 1990s, headed by bands like the Finnish group Nightwish, whose style was somewhere between hair metal and gothic chamber music. While the greater European scene created a number of interesting subgenres, most held only a limited appeal, at least compared to the popularity of eighties goth music and the electronic hybrids that dominated the clubs.

Goth Rises in the East

Goth took longer to catch on in Asia than in Europe and North America. Goth music was imported into both Japan and China in the 1980s and a few homegrown bands emerged, emulating the style. Goth really caught on in Asia in the mid-1990s, especially in Japan, which remained the uncontested leader of Asian goth culture into the twenty-first century.[24]

The Japanese embrace fetishism, both sexual and otherwise. There are hundreds of unusual interest groups in Japan, dedicated to interests ranging from Brazilian bossa nova to having intercourse with extraterrestrials. It seems only natural, therefore, that there would be a place in the Japanese heart for a brand of somewhat theatrical pop and rock music, tinged with romanticism.

After goth took hold in Japan, inspired by imported music, it developed in two very different directions. On one hand, an underground scene developed that focused on eighties-inspired goth music blended with "dark metal" and death rock. These Japanese goths listened to similar music and dressed similarly to their counterparts in western Europe and the United States.[25]

Japan also blended goth with one of its other, more unique genres, "visual kei" or "vijuaru kei," a style of Japanese rock (sometimes called J Rock) that involves elaborate costumes and makeup. Visual kei is enormously popular in Japan, and members of some of the biggest bands, like X JAPAN, Color, and Dead End, are superstar celebrities. The "androgynous look" is very big in visual kei, mirroring the goth aesthetic in other countries, though the music is usually not as dark and is more a blend of rock, punk, metal, and other genres.[26]

A few visual kei bands, including the tremendously popular Moi Dix Mois and Dir en Grey, tend more toward the goth side of things, producing music that is darker and more reminiscent of goth rock. Mana, a musician and designer from the dark visual kei band Malice Mizer, is one of the most popular musicians in visual kei. His biggest influence, however, is not through his music but rather the clothing style that he and his bands popularized and that he, as a designer, helped to bring into the boutiques of Harajuku Street. As will be discussed later, Mana's "Elegant Gothic Lolita" style not only became popular in Japan but was exported into Europe and the United States as well.[27]

The Japanese goth community is therefore divided between fans of the gothy visual kei and those who prefer a more Western goth sound. Some hardcore goth fans in Japan feel that visual kei bands like Malice Mizer are not really "goth," but a shallow, popularized version.[28]

Getting the Goth Out

Modern goths are spoiled for choice when it comes to music. Thanks to digital music exchange, the twenty-first-century goth has a wide variety of music at his or her disposal, from the catalog of early eighties bands through the most bizarre manifestations from the East. There are also Internet guides helping people to learn the history of goth music, and numerous discussion groups where fans can learn about the newest bands and the latest releases from around the world.

Before the Internet, most goth fans learned about new music by word of mouth. "Have you heard the new Christian Death single?" one friend might ask another, who might answer, "No, but I have this great Grave 45 album." Then the two friends would hug and, much to the chagrin of the record companies, share their music.

From the 1980s through the mid-1990s, goth albums were sold only through specialty stores or mail-order distributors. Mail-order catalogs were distributed in the back of fanzines, at concert venues, and through networks of friends. Throughout most of the 1980s and 1990s, mail-order companies were the lifeblood of the underground music scene, before Internet marketing and digital distribution made it possible for companies to sell limited-run recordings directly to the public.

One of the most successful distributors of goth music in the United States is Projekt: Darkwave, which began distributing music through mail order and small retail outlets in the late 1980s. Founder Sam Rosenthal, also the creator of the band Black Tape for a Blue Girl, started Projekt primarily as a way to distribute his own music. Rosenthal then moved on to releasing a few select recordings from other labels. It became clear, after a while, that there were a number of bands in need of a new label for distribution and, in 1989, Rosenthal founded his Darkwave label to fill the void.[29]

Between 1989 and 2010, Projekt moved from California, through Chicago, and then to New York, picking up a number of now prominent bands in the process like Lycia, Love Spirals Downward, and Voltaire. After years of working with small bands and record companies, Projekt developed a strong reputation among fans. "We've been in touch with many generations of fans of the genre," Rosenthal explained, "and we keep up with what they are looking for."[30] When Projekt releases an album or compilation, fans knew that it was going to be in keeping with the quality of previous releases and this trust helped Projekt and the artists they represented to reach larger audiences.

In the twenty-first century, successful record companies have shifted much of their business online. Record labels can release MP3s of singles, demos, and full albums directly to consumers. Online marketing not only allows companies to quickly and easily distribute their music but it allows labels to reach international audiences, a feat that was quite difficult in the era of mail-order marketing.

Many record companies also release compilation albums featuring samplings from their catalog. Compilations, whether homemade or distributed by labels, have long been one of the primary means by which fans learn about new artists. Coupling established artists with up-and-coming talent helps to get the word out about new bands, and labels attempt to attract old fans by offering exclusive singles and alternate versions.

MIX TAPE POWER

There is no better way for music aficionados to show their love than by making a mix tape. While it is a handy way to convey one's feelings through the artistry of others, it also spreads new music through the community, serving as user-generated marketing for the recording industry.

The Internet age hit the recording industry like a multimedia anvil. Not only did record companies have to scramble to gain a foothold in the electronic music sales industry, but they were also faced with increasingly stiff competition from independent artists and labels releasing their own music through online distribution networks. Independent recording and production has always played an important role in the industry, but technological advances have made it possible for artists to produce entire albums on a single home computer, achieving a level of complexity that would have required an entire studio in decades past.

The emerging digital music revolution brought about the death of many record labels and had the unfortunate effect of flooding the market with a brace of mediocre music. On the plus side, consumers reap the rewards with an unprecedented variety of music at their disposal.

Twenty-First-Century Gothoid

What is modern goth music? The question is difficult to answer, as the list of bands within the genre has become more and more diverse. Perhaps Sam Rosenthal encapsulates the situation best, saying "Goth is whatever the fans say it is."[31]

Traditional goth music still has an important place within the subculture, and albums from the initial four or five UK bands are virtually always present in any goth's collection. At the same time, there is always room for new subgenres. Dark Cabaret, a subgenre that blends gothy sounds with Weimar-era cabaret and vaudeville, is one example of a newer, innovative genre demonstrating how the goth aesthetic continues to evolve.

Some argue that goth music has stretched too far from its roots and that many of these modern subgenres have little or no connection to whatever goth is or once was. Still, there is overlap between subgenres, perhaps enough to state that, while each style is unique and independent, it at least has goth roots. "It's music that is dark, introspective, a bit moody and unsettling," says Rosenthal, though he admits that there is no good way to describe the genre as a whole.

The major division in the modern goth scene is between fans of the electro genres, like EBM, futurepop, and electro, and those who favor the older, more rock or new wave–centered styles. Divisions in musical tastes also translate into fashion choices and the kinds of clubs people tend to frequent, though there are many goths who enjoy the entire family of styles and may alternate between costumes and clubs depending on which venue is hosting the most interesting festivities.[32]

For the modern goth, there are multiple ways to view the current "scene." Some choose to view goth as a thing of the past, where the best music was made and played in the eighties and nineties, and the stuff that is going on now as little more than a hideous mutation. For others, the modern scene offers welcome variety and innovation. No matter how one chooses to look at it or whatever goth once was, there is still a "goth" thing in modern music, inspired by the past but fueled by contemporary aesthetics and interests. This wave of goth, like those that preceded it, is a legitimate part of a musical tradition that is older than any who now practice it, and which will inspire a new generation of listeners and musicians searching for the dark sound.

Notes

1. Paul Hodkinson, *Goth: Identity, Style and Subculture* (New York: Berg, 2002), 80–83.
2. Stephen Davies, *Musical Meaning and Expression* (Ithaca, NY: Cornell University Press, 1994), 160–65.
3. Josh Gunn, "Goth Music and the Inevitability of Genre," *Popular Music & Society* 23, no. 9 (1999): 31–50.
4. Interview Set 1, February–March 2010.
5. Personal interviews, February–March 2010.
6. Karen Kelly and Evelyn McDonnell, *Stars Don't Stand Still in the Sky: Music and Myth* (New York: Routledge, 1999), 50–52.

7. David Punter and Glennis Byron, *The Gothic* (Hoboken, NJ: Wiley-Blackwell, 1999), 63–70.

8. Lauren M. E. Goodlad and Michael Bibby, "Introduction," in *Goth: Undead Subculture*, ed. Lauren M. E. Goodland and Michael Bibby, 1–10 (Durham, NC: Duke University Press, 2007).

9. Ibid., 9–20.

10. Stephen Colegrave and Chris Sullivan, *Punk: The Definitive Record of a Revolution* (New York: Da Capo Press, 2001), 201.

11. Nancy Kilpatrick, *The Goth Bible: A Compendium for the Darkly Inclined* (New York: St. Martin's Griffin, 2004), 80–85.

12. Kristen Schilt, "Queens of the Damned: Women and Girls' Participation in Two Gothic Subcultures," in Goodlad and Bibby, *Goth*, 70–78.

13. David Richards, "Profile Rises for Prjekt's Black Tape," *Billboard*, November 21, 1998, 17.

14. Dave Thomson, *The Dark Reign of Gothic Rock* (London: Helter Skelter, 2002).

15. Interview with Pete Scathe, November 25, 2009.

16. Dunja Brill, *Goth Culture: Gender, Sexuality and Style* (New York: Berg, 2008), 7–8.

17. Ibid.

18. Personal conversation, March 24, 2010.

19. Dan Sicko, *Techno Rebels: The Renegades of Electronic Funk* (New York: Billboard Books), 135–46.

20. Brill, *Goth Culture*, 3–10.

21. Sicko, *Techno Rebels*, 140–45.

22. Brill, *Goth Culture*, 4–10.

23. Ibid., 5–6.

24. Ibid., 7–9.

25. Ibid., 9.

26. Tiffany Godoy and Ivan Vartanian, *Style Deficit Disorder: Harajuku Street Fashion, Tokyo* (San Francisco: Chronicle Books, 2007), 159.

27. Ibid., 159–62.

28. Brill, *Goth Culture*, 7.

29. Interview with Sam Rosenthal, March 9, 2010.

30. Ibid.

31. Ibid.

32. Interview with Pete Scathe, November 25, 2009.

CHAPTER THREE | Fashion, Bodies, and Beauty

Goth music is not common on popular radio stations, and goth magazines and other literature are usually found only by those who seek them out. Goth fashion, on the other hand, is the subculture's window dressing, and even those with no idea what goth is or who have never in their lives listened to goth music will notice the distinctive look on a passerby.

Modern goth fashion borrows elements from a variety of sources, both historical and current, and has distinct subgenres like "middle-ages goth," "Elegant Gothic Lolita," "vampire goth," and "cybergoth," each with its own unique spin on the basic model. There is an overarching aesthetic at play—exploring the beauty and allure of darker themes. From a simple monochrome palette to elaborate costumes inspired by horror and science fiction, goth fashion is a playground where individuals can explore alternate personas and hidden fantasies, and test the boundaries of the mainstream concept of beauty.

Over the years, the innovative and inventive goths have inspired numerous scholarly studies examining the social significance of their fashion, as well as a host of goth fashion magazines, a small cottage design industry, and even fashion shows in some of the world's most prestigious venues. Before goth hit the runway, however, it began with the simple complexity of black.

Black Beauty

Black is an achromatic shade, coming as close as possible (given the limitations of textile science) to absolute darkness. The color absorbs light rather than reflecting it, leaving behind only the contour and texture of the object draped within. Black has many cultural associations around the world; in some cultures it is the color of mourning, sadness, death, and evil, but alternately symbolizes elegance, strength, determination, and sex appeal.[1]

It is difficult to overestimate the importance of black to goth subculture. In Germany (the current capital of goth worldwide), the entire phenomenon is sometimes called "schwarz kultur" (black culture). In any language, from German "schwarz" to Japanese "goshikku," black is the center of the fashion palette.[2]

In western European culture, the color black is strongly associated with funerary rights and it is worn to show respect to the dead and their families. Before black was considered respectful, Europeans believed that by wearing black and covering the widow's face (as with a black veil), the restless spirits of the departed would be unable to find and haunt their living relatives.[3] Over the years, black gowns, suits, and veils took on alternate meanings and black became the color of mystery and serious intentions.

The association of black with evil is also strong in Western culture. Evil or sinister magic is called "black magic," and dark humor has been given the moniker "black comedy." Goths draw upon all of these associations, using black to create a look of mystery and sensuality, often with a tinge of the dangerous and playfully sinister.

Black has physical advantages when applied to clothing. It has a slimming effect on the silhouette, it creates contrast with other colors, and, if an individual remains still, it can block out the sun and heat.[4] There are disadvantages as well; black tends to display any light-colored debris or pet hair, it fades with repeated washing,

A black silk velvet dress by Thierry Mugler is on display during the press preview of "Gothic: Dark Glamour" at the Museum at FIT, September 4, 2008, in New York. (AP Photo/Mary Altaffer)

and, if an individual moves vigorously, black clothing will not allow heat to escape, leading more than one goth to collapse from heat stroke.

One of the most important elements of goth style is contrast. Descriptors like "striking" and "eye-catching" generally refer to this quality of an image, in which two different elements combine to create a visual hiccup. In aesthetics, this is called the "law of diversity," where features with contrasting qualities accentuate the nature of their differences, when viewed in association.[5]

Black is fantastic for contrast, and goths often use white, silver, or other bright colors to create contrast with their black base. Goth fashion in general is based almost more on contrast than absolute darkness, and it is contrast that provides the striking look achieved by a goth with white, pale skin, clothed in deep black.

Basic Goth

The basic goth look was developed largely by the musicians in the early goth bands. The archetype can be described as dark clothing, dark hair, and dark makeup contrasting with pale white skin. Early goth album covers were almost always shot in black-and-white, but even in full color the early goths tried to appear as close to monochrome as clothing and makeup would allow.[6]

Punk rock fashion and goth fashion developed simultaneously and have many elements in common, including a preference for ripped and tattered clothing, religious-themed jewelry and spiked accessories, and body modifications like piercings and tattoos. Punk fashion was more of a DIY movement, utilizing found clothing, faux military apparel, and rock T-shirts.[7] In contrast to the punks' chaotic style, the goths are often described as better "put together," preferring a more meditated and elegant approach.[8]

Over the years, as new versions of goth style emerged, the basic uniform endured and is still accepted in goth clubs around the world. For men, trench coats, tight black pants, and boots are basic. For women, black stockings, dresses, and silver jewelry.

Hairstyles have always been very important to the goth image. In the beginning, goth hair was similar to the punk and/or new wave look: spiky, black-dyed creations and flat, mopey locks occasionally with portions of the head shaved, à la the punk look. In the 1990s, dreadlocks became more common, sometimes with splashes of color to highlight the contrast. Men also began wearing their hair longer, and this became a standard for the goth male.

In the 1990s, colored clothing and accessories became more common in goth style, even bright pink, which was once considered

THE DREADED LOCKS

Dreadlocks are clumps of matted hair that first originated in Africa. Though linked to Rastafarianism, dreadlocks have become popular in the West as an alternative style statement. Hairstylists sometimes use synthetic implants to give a person "instant locks," which come in any color including neon yellow and other unnatural shades.

the antithesis of goth.[9] Another change was the addition of fetish-inspired clothing, including PVC pants, skirts, shirts, and dresses. While goth culture has always been less overtly sexual than fetish culture, the two often come into contact, sharing both the same basic hours of operation (late nights) and the same spaces, primarily clubs that are open-minded enough to welcome both groups.[10]

Goth fashion changed in concert, both literally and figuratively, with goth music. The integration of electronica led to overlaps with rave or club culture, including fluorescent clothing and hair, the addition of glitter, and mini-backpacks. More metal minded goths adopted the heavier combat boots and leather, spiked accessories characteristic of the "metal heads." As goth expanded in Europe and Asia, new stylistic elements were added, blending genres as disparate as renaissance fashion and Japanese anime.[11]

Many goths move between genres, in terms of both music and fashion. An American goth might attend an eighties night dressed in basic attire one night and then switch to fangs and Victorian accoutrements for a vampire-goth outing the next.[12] Some goths, often called "corporate goths," adopt a modest version of the style for work, still wearing the characteristic black but removing piercings and jewelry so as not to alarm the "normal folk" at their day jobs, then switch to more elaborate costumes for postwork festivities.[13]

The Significance of Goth Style

In any subculture, clothing and body modifications are among the most important signifiers of belonging. Fashion always combines personal preference and conformity, and always involves some element of communication. Goths adopting the style communicate their belonging with other goths while simultaneously making a clear statement to those outside that they absolutely DO NOT belong to the mainstream.[14]

In interviews, most goths claim "personal preference" and "individuality" as among the highest goals of goth fashion. Despite this claim, analyses have found that the culture tends to be "highly conformist" in style.[15] Individuals are free to mix and match, add distinctive or unique elements, or even create "transgressive" styles that

INVERTED MESSAGES

The inverted or "upside-down" cross originally signified the Christian Saint Peter, who was reportedly crucified hanging upside-down. Anti-Christian groups, like Satanists and cultists, adopted the symbol to represent the "opposite" of Christianity. Some modern wearers of Peter's Cross simply think it looks cool.

utilize elements from "outside" cultures. This is how individuality is maintained; however, an individual who strays too far from the basic mold will likely be viewed either as "trying too hard" or simply as an outsider.[16]

Sociologists have described the fashion of certain subcultures, like hippies, goths, punks, and beatniks, as "subversive style," serving as a type of "symbolic violation of the social order."[17] This type of symbolic rebellion can be highly effective as it immediately sets the wearer apart and provides an obvious, visual commentary on the larger culture.

Wearing a crucifix on one's neck coupled with a pentagram, for instance, is in one sense simply a fashion choice while it may simultaneously have a much different meaning to an onlooker who ascribes sacred, personal meanings to those symbols. On the other hand, communicating distaste with the social order through fashion can reduce protest to a mere "shopping preference," as individuals readily engage in consumerism while at the same time wanting to distance themselves from consumer culture and the individuals who follow its central vein.[18]

The Feminine Mystique

One of the most debated and studied aspects of goth style is the veneration of the "androgynous" look for male goths, characterized by those having thin bodies and faces with pale skin and little body hair.[19] This is not to say that goths will not accept people who are overweight or have darker skin or muscled bodies, but males with more effeminate forms have a distinct advantage, including increased attention from both potential romantic partners and friends.

Early goth icons were usually men with a somewhat effeminate appearance, and the same can be said for the artists who inspired early goths, like David Bowie and other glam rockers. Feminine clothing, such as skirts and fishnet stockings, became more popular with goth men in the 1990s, as did more elaborate makeup and other traditionally feminine aspects of style.[20] Certain modes of behavior, including being (openly) preoccupied with appearance and utilizing professional hair, nail, and cosmetic services, are accepted in male goth culture, whereas in the mainstream they are generally considered feminine concerns.

This aspect of goth culture has created a misconception within the mainstream that most goth men are homosexual. While effeminate style is held in high esteem, few goths describe themselves as gay or lesbian and only a small number report having engaged in bisexual relationships.[21] Goth culture is overwhelmingly heterosexual, and the male preference for androgynous style seems to be based more on the transgression of gender norms than on a desire to fill a female role in romantic relationships.

Sociologist Dunja Brill, herself a longtime participant in both the German and British goth scenes, described goth as a "cult of femininity," because both males and females aspire to achieve a "feminized" form of beauty. Gender transgression is supported in males, but the gate does not swing both ways and similar behavior is discouraged in females. Women are strongly discouraged from adopting masculine or even average dress and are instead generally expected to dress in such a way as to enhance their femininity.[22]

Though most goths describe themselves as heterosexual, they are accepting and generally supportive of gay and lesbian behavior. In fact, goths often express sympathy and fondness for almost any marginalized group, from LGBT (lesbian, gay, bisexual, and transsexual) to racial minorities and just about any group on the social periphery.[23] It is perhaps because goths often feel like outcasts that they strongly identify with these groups. Despite their sympathies, goth culture around the world is largely Caucasian and relatively homogeneous, with few minorities represented within their ranks.

When asked about the popularity of the androgynous look, respondents claimed that goths wanted to free themselves from sexism, female objectification, and other ills commonly ascribed to masculine dominance.[24] Some also claim that gender is not important in their relationships and that they form bonds based on personality, rather than relying on attraction.[25] Seemingly, goths have developed an idealized concept of culture, in which gender is not nearly as important a factor in the formation of interpersonal relationships. Sociological studies indicate that, in practice, the "genderless" environment is never fully realized as sex and gender roles continue to play a dominant role in goth culture.

Even if genderlessness is more fantasy than reality, goths have fostered a culture in which many females and those with alternative sexual preferences often feel empowered. Even when goth women choose to adopt clothes designed to accentuate their sex appeal, they do so within a culture at least partially removed from the objectification that women face in other environments.

Within some of goth's sub-sub-cultures, like "electrogoth," "cybergoth," and "deathrock," traditional masculinity is more in evidence and traditional male-female relationships tend to be the norm. Thus is seems that femininity is not universal in goth, but rather the freedom to express femininity is open to both men and women, and is often embraced within the culture at large.

Inspiration, Innovation, and Authenticity

Goth fashion draws from a variety of influences. Siouxsie Sioux, who inspired a generation of goth women, crafted ensembles that were part S&M gear, part paramilitary, and part Ziggy Stardust. Compared to Sioux, most of the other early goth bands were fairly conservative, preferring the simplicity of long black coats, flat dark hair, and perhaps some white foundation, for that lovely undead look.[26]

From the beginning, goth garb was about being seen and going out. The clubs were the place to show off one's best ensembles, as well as a source of inspiration for those new to the look. Appreciation of each other's clothing, hair, and makeup is a conversation starter and often leads to friendships. As goths share information, the names of goth-friendly shops and designers spread throughout the community, creating an underground fashion network.

For super-dressy events, some goths integrate elements of period attire, especially Victorian clothing. Women might wear period-inspired ball gowns, corsets, parasols, and veils, while men wear long frock coats, top hats, and other period-specific accessories.

Goth period attire generally resembles the "Victorian Cult of Mourning," a fashion bubble that gripped British society in the early 1860s. Following the death of Prince Albert in December 1861, Queen Victoria fell into a period of deep depression and mourning. Victoria decreed that all visitors to the palace should wear black head to toe, at all social functions, and she herself continued to dress in black for the rest of her life.

When the queen said "black," members of the court said, "Yes mum," and proceeded to put their tailors and jewelers to work, crafting fashionable clothing and accessories suitable for mourning but with a somber elegance. Throughout the next decade, mourning chic filtered from court to the peasantry and became part of mainstream fashion.[27]

While black trench coats and pants can be purchased nearly anywhere, nineteenth-century formal wear and more unique items can be difficult to acquire. Specialty vendors and independent clothing makers fill this niche, often creating fashions aimed specifically at goth clientele. As individuality is highly sought after within goth circles, the opportunity to supplement one's clothing collection with unique items attracts many goths to specialty designers.

Philadelphia-based designers Psydde Delicious and Amy Schmitz, of Delicious Corsets, produce and sell a variety of elegant corsets, often to goth clients. Delicious Corsets, which are designed to be worn outside the clothing, are inspired by historical designs but flavored by contemporary fashion. Another specialty vendor, designer Norie Ayukawa, produces jewelry under the company name Hyde's Vice, featuring skulls and other horror-themed designs and inspired by turn-of-the-century jewelry styles. Items like those produced by Ayukawa and Delicious Corsets would be a rare find, even in a boutique that carries period clothing. The demand for accessories and clothing to fit the goth palette has therefore created a market for designers whose own artistic sensibilities tend towards this bizarre and unusual aesthetic.

It is nearly impossible for any goth to get *all* of his or her clothing from designers, but goths who take pride in their clothing spend considerable time and money shopping. Finding stores, boutiques, and thrift shops that offer items appropriate to the look is part of the ritual of being goth. Friends gather to shop, helping one another choose appropriate attire and keeping in touch with their community by visiting shops frequented by other local goths.[28]

The Hot Topic chain of retail stores, found in shopping malls across America, caters to alternative clothing and costume aficionados. Hot Topic offers a number of items that can be called "goth-inspired," though most within the subculture consider Hot Topic to be a place where "poseurs" shop. Some even use the derogatory "mall goth" sobriquet to refer to those whose idea of goth comes from Hot Topic and similar boutiques. However, for some young people, living in smaller communities with limited retail resources, Hot Topic and similar chains are the closest they can get to "real" goth apparel. Even reputable goths might occasionally snag an item from Hot Topic, though they may not tell anyone else where they got it.

In some sociological theories, subcultures begin to lose their subcultural status once their music, fashion, and other characteristic products have been co-opted by the larger culture. Participants lose interest in their subculture as it is subsumed by the mainstream and killed by popularity. As soon as new members begin flocking to the scene attracted only by the superficial elements and without adhering to any of the underlying motivations, the subculture is in danger of death by overexposure.

While goth fashion and music have become sufficiently popular to inspire imitation, the culture refuses to succumb to malignant popularity. This is partially because, while some elements of goth have gone mainstream, authentic goth culture takes place behind closed doors in venues that attract only those with serious interest, and remain largely unseen by superficial followers. While a generation of teenagers shops at Hot Topic and listens to whatever goth-inspired rock appears on radio stations, there has always been an underground aspect to the culture where innovation and authenticity keep the subculture one step ahead of its mainstream caricatures.

Goth Gets Around

The basic goth fashion formula is similar around the world, but there are scenes in which this mold has evolved in new, sometimes radically different directions. While all goth styles have a touch of dark romance in common, there are many different ways of approaching this idea. The following are some of the more unusual and interesting subgenres of goth fashion.

Cybergoth

Imagine traveling to the distant future, a time when robots and humans coexist and perhaps even extraterrestrials have made an appearance or two on Earth. Once there, you travel into some backstreet club and realize that goths have survived the ages and, what's more, they've become half-robot undead creatures, who still like electronic music! This is sort of what cybergoth is like.

The cybergoth scene developed in Europe as DJs began blending goth rock and electronica. The basic cybergoth look combines typical undead goth attire with futuristic elements, like PVC armbands outfitted with circuit boards or steel plates, making it appear as if the wearer is part machine. Other popular accessories include industrial goggles, faux military gear, helmets, and heavy work boots. There are also outfits made to look as if the wearer has undergone some form of cybernetic surgery, perhaps opening the chest or head to implant circuitry.

Many cybergoths have been inspired by the "steampunk" genre of fiction, which envisions worlds in which steam and coal technology still dominate and are used to fuel fantastic machines, like steam-powered computers or coal-powered robots. The genre combines romanticized historical fiction—often with stories taking place in Victorian England or early nineteenth-century America—with more typical science fiction themes, such as robots, futuristic military technology, and space travel. Goth and steampunk share many aesthetic elements and literary researcher Michael Du Plessis sums up the relationship, saying that a steampunk is basically a goth who wears brown instead of black.[29]

Similarly, the fiction genre known as "cyberpunk" involves future clashes between misfits and social outcasts, struggling against dominant government or corporate forces in a future where humans can enhance their bodies with robotic implants. Drawn from books like William Gibson's *Neuromancer* and *Johnny Mnemonic*, cyberpunk has also become a source of inspiration for many in the cybergoth environment.

The heroes of both steampunk and cyberpunk novels are often depicted as rebels, outcasts, and freedom fighters. In fantasy worlds where the population is controlled by powerful and generally evil forces (often depicted as multinational corporations), the protagonists fight for the rights of the little people, helping to free the masses from the shadow of technological domination.

While predictions of the future are usually more wrong than right, the clash between human and machine is very much in evidence in modern society and fueled by paranoia over virtual terrorism, cyber crime, and the ultimate, unforeseen consequences of our culture's ever-increasing dependence on computers. Cybergoth fashion brings versions of this fantastic dystopian future to life and conjures a romanticized underground resistance to the painful, imagined struggles that might define humanity's future.

Vampire Goths and Other Fantasy Creatures

Vampire goths are their own special breed within the subculture. Taking inspiration from horror fiction, these goths dress and sometimes attempt to behave like vampire-esque creatures, whether preferring traditional Dracula chic or some type of futuristic vampire-alien hybrid. Once a peripheral style within the subculture, vampire play has become common in many goth circles. One of the largest goth gatherings in the United States, the quarterly Dracula's Ball in Philadelphia, is a vampire-themed party at which many of the more than 1,000 attendees attempt to cultivate the vampire goth look in one form or another.

Films and books often serve as the beginning of a new fashion craze within the subculture. After the release of *Edward Scissorhands* in 1990, more than one goth was inspired to try out a goth-meets-frankenstein-meets-fetish look. The film versions of Bram Stoker's *Dracula* in 1992 and Anne Rice's *Interview with a Vampire* in 1994 also inspired trends within the goth community, popularizing the Victorian-vampire-meets-modern-clubgoer theme.[30]

In addition to clothing, some more dedicated vampire goths purchase dental implants to give them vampire-style fangs. Permanent, professionally fit dental caps of this kind may cost from around $1,000 to more than $5,000 including having them attached, placing

---

PERMANENTLY HORNY

Those interested in the extreme devilish look do not have to stop at filed incisors. Body artists also offer horn implants, small protuberances of Teflon inserted under the skin of the forehead. It is even possible to give a person a serpentine forked tongue with surgical modification.

---

them beyond the reach of many goths. For an affordable alternative, there are numerous companies offering temporary acrylic fangs that allow a goth to play vampire without committing to permanent modification. Another popular way to up the supernatural look is to purchase custom contact lenses. The Oregon-based company 9SFX offers a variety of theatrical contact lenses costing between $100 and $400, including lenses styled after vampires, zombies, aliens, and a variety of other unusual looks.

Those who take the vampire or supernatural look too far risk ridicule within the general goth community, as it can be seen as "trying too hard" or just plain silly. However, a bit of vampire flair thrown into a goth ensemble, especially if handled with some degree of humor, has become a generally accepted part of goth fashion.

Vampires are not the only supernatural beings that appeal to members of the culture, and some goths opt for looks fashioned after other types of inhuman creatures. There have always been some goths who go for an undead look, inspired by zombies and similar monsters, while others prefer a more feminine or magical approach, dressing in a combination of goth and fairy or dark wizard attire. While Dark fairies, wizards, and vampires may not be common in most goth clubs, they do constitute one of the more unique and interesting offshoots of the style.

Elegant Gothic Lolitas

Elegant Gothic Lolita, or EGL, is a fashion trend pioneered among Japan's visual kei scene, a style of music that blends rock, goth, punk, and theatrical performance. EGL is an offshoot of baby doll fashion; the creation of adult-sized dresses and other pieces of clothing based on the outfits made for children's toy dolls. EGL aficionados wear twisted baby doll designs in dark colors, with decorative elements and accessories inspired by horror and dark fiction. Poufy black dresses with white lace trim are central to the style, as well as a variety of horror-themed accessories, like parasols in the shape of bat wings, leather backpacks shaped like coffins, and many other items resembling some sort of undead childhood nightmare.

Mana, the lead singer of the visual kei band Moi Dix Mois, is one of the originators of the EGL style. In 1999, Mana founded the fashion label, Moi-même-Moitié, which produces clothing and accessories in both Elegant Gothic Lolita and the related Elegant Gothic Aristocrat style, which is inspired by historical Victorian and Elizabethan clothing, again mixed with the more typical gothic aesthetic.[31]

Many Japanese fashionistas who don EGL designs do not listen to goth music and sometimes do not even like visual kei. The EGL style has become a fashion phenomenon unto itself, as EGL fans don their latest additions and gather in fashion-forward neighborhoods, like Tokyo's Harajuku Street, to admire each other's fashions while passing tourists snap photos.

Elements of Gothic Lolita style have become evident in the European and U.S. goth scenes as well, some transported by Japanese immigrants and some inspired by photos of the elaborate Lolitas in Japan. Even if the style is not one of the mainstays of Western goth, it has made a mark and most goths at least know what Gothic Lolita is and have seen someone attempting a version of the style.

Gothic Continuum

Goth fashion, like nearly every other element of the goth style, represents an attempt (or rather many different attempts) to capture the strange and delicate appeal that occurs at the junction of horror and romance. From Victorian lace to futuristic zombie robots, each of the subgenres can be traced back to this very basic aesthetic, the beauty of the strange, dark, and unsettling.

Goths from around the world may share a basic similarity in their wiring, pushing them further toward the shadowy side of fashion and away from mainstream aesthetic sensibilities. While this attraction to the dark and mysterious is widespread, most shy away from it, preferring the safety of mainstream fashion and lifestyle. Goths refuse this path, preferring to indulge in their fascination with the bizarre and otherworldly, to dress and become, if only for hours each night, a person who lives in an alternate world, where things are a little more twisted and a lot more interesting.

Notes

1. Edith Anderson Feisner, *Colour: How to Use Colour in Art and Design* (London: Laurence King, 2006), 120–30.
2. Dunja Brill, *Goth Culture: Gender, Sexuality and Style* (New York: Berg, 2008), 1–7.
3. Charles Panati, *Panati's Extraordinary Origins of Everyday Things* (New York: Harper Perennial, 1989), 36–37.
4. Nancy Kilpatrick, *The Goth Bible: A Compendium for the Darkly Inclined* (New York: St. Martin's Griffin, 2004), 38–39.
5. Langdon S. Thompson, *Aesthetic Manual* (Charleston, SC: BiblioBazaar, 2009), 20–23.
6. Paul Hodkinson, *Goth: Identity, Style and Subculture* (New York: Berg, 2002), 40–50.
7. Malcolm Barnard, *Fashion as Communication* (New York: Routledge, 2002), 137.
8. Catherin Spooner, *Fashioning Gothic Bodies* (Manchester, UK: Manchester University Press, 2004), 159–90.
9. Hodkinson, *Goth*, 38–40.
10. Jeffrey Andrew Weinstock, "Gothic Fetishism," in *Goth: Undead Subculture*, ed. Lauren M. E. Goodlad and Michael Bibby, 390 (Durham, NC: Duke University Press, 2007).
11. Tiffany Godoy and Ivan Vartanian, *Style, Deficit, Disorder: Harajuku Street Fashion, Tokyo* (San Francisco: Chronicle Books, 2007), 159–62.
12. Interview with Pete Scathe, November 25, 2009.
13. Hodkinson, *Goth*, 30–50.
14. Brill, *Goth Culture*, 37.
15. Ibid., 40–43.
16. Hodkinson, *Goth*, 40–50.
17. Brill, *Goth Culture*, 22.
18. Ibid., 22–30.
19. Hodkinson, *Goth*, 30–40.
20. Spooner, *Fashioning Gothic*, 60–75.
21. Brill, *Goth Culture*, 122.
22. Ibid., 37.
23. Rebecca Schraffenberger, "This Modern Goth (Explains Herself)," in Goodlad and Bibby, *Goth*, 125.

24. Personal interviews, Club Shampoo, November 28, 2009.
25. Brill, *Goth Culture*, 40–47.
26. Valerie Steele, *Fetish: Fashion, Sex and Power* (New York: Oxford University Press, 1997), 37.
27. Karen Halttunen, *Confidence Men and Painted Women: A Study of Middle-Class Culture in America* (New Haven, CT: Yale University Press, 1986), 125–30.
28. Hodkinson, *Goth*, 61–70.
29. Interview with Lauren M. E. Goodlad, May 17, 2010.
30. Kilpatrick, *Goth Bible*, 25.
31. Steele, *Dark Glamour*, 52–56.

CHAPTER FOUR

Goth Fiction and Fantasy

Goth culture is creative. Started by musicians, fueled by writers and filmmakers, and attended by designers, painters, sculptors, and a host of would-be creatives, goth culture is deeply rooted in a tradition of artistic expression. The original gothic thing was expressed through architecture and literature, while music and film are the twentieth- and twenty-first-century additions, providing visual and aural re-creations and reinventions of the aesthetic for a new generation.

Many of the quintessential goth films and books were not created by goths, but by artists outside the culture. Even so, the average goth is probably more driven by his or her artistic tastes than the average person, and many are avid consumers of the arts, not just music and fashion but also literature, film, and other genres. Goths who manage to make a major impact are usually musicians, and occasionally writers and visual artists.

Gothic Literature Meets Goth Literature

Gothic literature (also called "gothic fiction" or "gothic horror") is a subgenre of fiction that began in the 1740s, combining the genres of horror and romance. Early works like Edward Young's poem *Night Thoughts* (1742) and *Treatise on Vampires and Revenants: The Phantom World* (1746) by Dom Augustine Calmet helped set the tone for the genre. Horace Walpole's 1765 novel, *The Castle of Otranto: A Gothic Story*, is often cited as the first true work of gothic fiction and played a major role in inspiring later writers.[1] Gothic fiction was immensely popular for decades, repeatedly reinvigorated by the publication of what became seminal works in the genre, like Mary Wollstonecraft Shelley's *Frankenstein* (1818) and Bram Stoker's *Dracula* (1897).[2]

Whether written in the eighteenth or nineteenth century, most gothic novels share certain basic characteristics. A gothic tale is typically set in a lonely and forbidding environment, like a medieval Middle Eastern or European village. Many gothic novels also feature, somewhat predictably, gothic architecture. Many gothic novelists use architecture almost as another character, providing opportunities for long, ominous descriptions of the scenery.

There is almost always an element of the supernatural, whether ghosts or the afterlife or evil creatures, in any gothic novel. There is also a common thread of terror, whether wrought by some supernatural enemy or just a good old-fashioned murderer. Finally, all gothic novels involve love, and not the kind that ends with the words "happily ever after," but the kind where everything goes wrong and ends in sadness, despair, regret, and longing.[3]

Gothic literature was, and remains, a major source of inspiration for modern goths. From the beginning, goth bands were inspired by images of classic monsters and gothic settings. So too the combination of horror and romance (or at least sadness and longing) became an important part of the emerging subculture.

Gothic fiction spread from England to the United States, where it inspired "southern gothic fiction," books set in a deeply romanticized southern landscape where willow trees and dilapidated colonial mansions harbor dark secrets. This genre had enough continuing appeal to spark twenty-first-century versions, including *The Southern Vampire Mysteries* (2001–10), a series of books (commonly known as the "Sookie Stackhouse novels") written by author Charlaine Harris that inspired the HBO television series *True Blood* (2009–10).[4]

While these modern works of romance and fiction are not generally included in the official confines of "gothic literature," the themes are the same—love, loss, supernatural forces, spirituality, and a variety of other poignant issues in an environment drenched with mystery, horror, and suspense.

Vampire literature is one of the most successful subgenres of horror and has important ties to goth culture. As mentioned earlier, a significant number of goths tend toward vampire fetishism, especially in their fashion choices, and these goths are often inspired by vampire fiction. Anne Rice's vampire novels, including *Interview with a Vampire* (1976), *The Vampire Lestat* (1985), and the more contemporary *Blood Canticle* (2003), were embraced by many goths, some of whom were inspired to add a bit of Victorian vampire flare to their goth costumes.[5]

Vampire literature comes in a variety of forms and often inspires films. While some authors present vampires in a traditional gothic setting, others choose to throw in science fiction elements, placing their vampires in the distant future or on other planets. Some authors cast them as heroes, others as villains, and many choose something in between, portraying vampires as basically good people who have been forced to act in unsavory ways. A few authors have even used vampires as protagonists in teen romance novels.[6]

Modern gothic fiction includes not only traditional novels but also comic books and graphic novels. The graphic literature industry has come a long way from marketing primarily to children and a few childlike adults. Modern graphic novels come in adult varieties, containing sex, graphic violence, and themes not intended or even remotely suitable for children. In the eighties and nineties, adult-themed comics began carrying parental warnings.

As many aspects of the overall goth aesthetic are visual, goth horror is particularly suited to the graphic format. Neil Gaiman, author of both traditional books and graphic novels, has become especially popular with goth audiences. Gaiman's writings, especially his *Sandman* series and the novel *Coraline*, became goth classics, both for their visual style and for Gaiman's characters, who often echo elements of the goth attitude.[7]

Dark humor is another popular subgenre within gothic fiction. Books like Voltaire's *Oh My Goth!* (2002) and his graphic novel *Oh My Goth: Humans Suck* (2000) have developed a strong following in the subculture.[8] There are many examples of novels in this vein,

JAPANIMAE

The subgenre of Japanese animation called "manga" often features supernatural themes and dark stories. This style of comic and film gained popularity with Western audiences in the 1980s. Several popular manga films, including *Vampire Hunter D* and *Ninja Scroll*, have gained cult status within the goth subculture.

designed to make readers laugh and cringe simultaneously. While some goths take themselves very, very seriously, many in the subculture recognize the humor of a culture in which "back-combed" hair and vampire fangs have become commonplace. The dark humor genre appeals to those goths who do not take themselves too seriously and are willing to acknowledge the more lighthearted side of the subculture's obsession with drama and death.

Some of the most innovative examples of modern gothic fiction have been developed by a new generation of women writers, using goth-esque themes and sexuality to create unique and compelling stories. Author Poppy Z. Brite became well known to goth audiences in the 1990s after the publication of her first book *Lost Souls* (1992). Brite's early novels involved vampires, which Brite imagined not as twisted or evil humans, but rather as a separate species that evolved alongside humanity. Brite often used openly gay characters as her primary protagonists and explored sexual and intimate relationships in graphic detail.

Another popular author is Storm Constantine, a British sci-fi and fantasy author whose *Wraeththu* series of novels are now considered modern classics of goth fiction. Like Brite, Constantine's characters are often grappling not only with supernatural drama but also with complicated issues involving sexual identity and intimacy. Constantine has explored homosexual relationships, transgendered characters, and hermaphrodites in her books, using the genre not only to write about spiritual themes but also to comment on the lives of those whose urges, desires, and perhaps biological makeup place them outside mainstream acceptance.[9]

Since the beginning of the science fiction/fantasy genre, authors and filmmakers have embraced the opportunity to use their fantasy

INTERRACIAL SPACE

The series *Star Trek* broadcast the first interracial kiss on television in 1968. To appease conservative viewers, it was explained that both crew members were "forced to kiss" while under telekinetic control. Despite these caveats, producer Gene Roddenberry's intention was to indicate that, in the future, interracial relations would no longer be taboo.

and futuristic worlds as a setting for morality plays, in which the author can explore sensitive contemporary issues like racism, sexuality, xenophobia, and mortality. This can be clearly seen in the writing for popular television programs. For example, the science fiction program *Star Trek*, which began airing in the 1960s, was able to explore issues like race relations by shifting its stories to other planets or often simply by saying that, in this imagined version of the future, race relations will be vastly different.[10] Similarly, the British science fiction program *Torchwood* centers around an openly bisexual protagonist whose sexual behavior is explained by implying, though never directly stating, that, in the future, humans will abandon their prejudices regarding homosexuality and heterosexuality and will instead simply have sex with anyone they are attracted to, be it a man, woman, or alien.[11]

Modern goth fantasy writers follow this tradition, using fantasy worlds to talk about pressing, uncomfortable issues, but tend to take a more direct approach than writers of mainstream fantasy. Writers like Brite and Constantine use graphic, often journalistic descriptions of sex, violence, and torture juxtaposed with fantastic creatures and fantasy worlds. This approach pushes the boundaries of using fantasy to reflect reality, conjuring the darkest shadows of the modern world through an otherworldly lens.

Goth Goes to the Movies

Early goth musicians were certainly inspired by film imagery, especially early horror films from the 1930s and 1940s starring Boris Karloff, Bela Lugosi, and the Lon Chaneys (Sr. and Jr.). Ominous scenery, often involving castles, cathedrals, and laboratories, set the stage for these dramatic (often to comedic levels) explorations of fear, violence, and tragedy, which "make you confront your own fragile mortality."[12]

An early pioneer of the horror film genre was Georges Méliès, a French filmmaker who experimented with multiple exposures and time-lapse photography to create "special effects." His 1896 film *Le Manoir Du Diable* (House of the Devil) is perhaps the earliest horror film on record, depicting a journey into a foreboding castle where we meet Mephistopheles and then see him banished when confronted with a Christian cross.[13]

The expressionist films of the 1920s were the next great step in horror cinema. These included director Robert Wiene's *The Cabinet of Dr. Caligari* (1919)[14] and F. W. Murnau's unlicensed adaptation of Bram Stoker's *Dracula*, the silent film *Nosferatu* (1922). Images from both films became symbolic of the genre as a whole, and both films inspired (and continue to inspire) countless filmmakers and writers.[15]

From German expressionism, the big Hollywood studios took over and, with the help of a small group of brilliant actors and directors, brought gothic literature to life. Film versions of *Frankenstein* (1931)[16] and *Dr. Jekyll and Mr. Hyde* (1931)[17] helped to create a mini horror craze among moviegoers. This was in no small part due to the charisma of actors like Bela Lugosi and Boris Karloff, whose performances in the roles of iconic literary monsters captivated audiences and helped to create a new hunger for horror and suspense.

While the horror film genre thrived in the 1970s and 1980s, goths have a special affection for the feel and imagery of the earlier classics. When Bauhaus released their now classic song "Bela Lugosi's Dead" in 1979, the cover art for the single featured images taken from *The Cabinet of Dr. Caligari*. Everything about the song, from Peter Murphy's lyrical delivery to the arrangement of the cover art, became symbolic of the "classic goth style," including the association between goth music and the early horror films.

Creating one of the gothiest movie moments of all time, director Tony Scott cast Bauhaus in his 1983 vampire film, *The Hunger*, in which the band was depicted playing their hit song on stage, combined with images of goth inspiration David Bowie as a vampire. The film was a critical failure but an instant cult classic, and the combination of vampire Bowie and Bauhaus was enshrined as a quintessential moment in the history of the subculture.[18]

Vampire films deserve a special mention in the category of goth movies. From the early vampire films like *Nosferatu* and Bela Lugosi's *Dracula* (1931), vampire films have inspired goth art and fashion. Researchers studying the goth scene in the 1990s noted that, after the release of the 1992 film version of *Dracula* and the 1994 film adaptation of Anne Rice's *Interview with a Vampire*, vampire fashion became much more common among male goths.[19] Even action-oriented films like the *Blade* trilogy appear in some goths' lists of favorite films.

Another vampire film that features prominently among goth favorites is *Shadow of the Vampire* (2000), by director E. Elias Merhige, a fictionalized portrayal of the filming of the 1922 film *Nosferatu*. In the film, director F. W. Murnau (played by John Malkovich) discovers a vampire named Max Schreck (played by Willem Dafoe) and casts him in his film. Being an actual vampire, Schreck produces a remarkably believable performance, but also decides to kill and eat some of the director's supporting staff.

Director Tim Burton is perhaps the quintessential goth filmmaker of the modern age. Burton's films capture the goth sensibility in terms of style and often subject matter, but presented in such a way that the films speak to a much larger audience. In interviews, Burton often references the classic horror and science fiction films as his primary motivation for getting into design and filmmaking.[20]

Burton's 1990 film *Edward Scissorhands* is a gothic fantasy, presenting the delicately featured Johnny Depp in the role of a goth Frankenstein-esque character abandoned by his creator and searching for belonging and love in an alien world of superficial suburban plasticity. *Scissorhands* is so full of symbolism that the plot almost takes the backseat. Burton created a literal interpretation of adolescent isolation, giving his hero razor sharp blades for fingers so that he has no choice but to remain alone or destroy anything he touches.[21]

Another goth favorite from Burton's catalog was *The Nightmare before Christmas* (1993), which brought the shadowy aesthetic to bear in a children's story. Images from *Nightmare*, including those of the story's protagonist Jack Skellington, a singing, skeletal hero, are sometimes seen on T-shirts in goth clubs.[22]

Actor Johnny Depp, left, and director Tim Burton pose for a photograph in West Hollywood, California, December 5, 2007. (AP Photo/Kevork Djansezian)

During the 1990s and 2000s, as public awareness of goth culture became more widespread, more filmmakers began using goth characters in their films. Most goth characters in films are young women, perhaps because mainstream audiences more readily accept the feminized goth look on women than on men. In Burton's 1990 film *Beetlejuice*, the character of Lydia, played by actress Winona Ryder, is one of the earliest film portrayals of a goth, or at least the general public opinion of what goths are like.

EFFECTS OF HORROR

To make monsters come alive, Hollywood studios invest billions in effects development. Technicians use the term "visual effects" for effects added postproduction, which includes the now ubiquitous CGI (computer-generated imagery) process. The term "special effects" is used for preproduction effects, including animatronic characters, puppets, and makeup.

Lydia is depicted as an intelligent, creative, and reclusive teenager, at odds with her father and stepmother and feeling as if she does not belong in the family. Her dramatic sense of isolation is presented in a humorous way by Burton, who even inserts a scene where Lydia is contemplating suicide and composing a note that begins "I am alone," before throwing it away and deciding that it would be better to lead with "I am *utterly* alone."

Lydia's dialogue is riddled with jokes poking fun at typical goth morbidity. When told she is allowed to have a darkroom in their new house, Lydia replies, "My whole life is a darkroom." Later, when she reads from a book saying that humans tend to ignore things that are strange and unusual, she says, "I myself *am* strange and unusual."[23]

Over the next two decades, a variety of filmmakers used goth girl caricatures in their films, often as comic relief, lightening the mood with sarcastic quips. The sassy goth girl can be found in films like *The Butterfly Effect* (2004), *Blair Witch 2: Book of Shadows* (2000), *Bride of Chucky* (1998), *8mm* (1999), *Queen of the Damned* (2002), and *Strangeland* (1998). The children's animated television program *Teen Titans*, which aired from 2003 to 2006, featured a gothy superheroine named Raven, portrayed as a wickedly sarcastic and often shy character whose powers included telekinetic and telepathic abilities (virtually every goth's dream) blended with some good old-fashioned magical incantations.

Common Themes for Uncommon Minds

Whether in film or in print, goth audiences respond to certain types of characters, certain settings, and certain underlying themes. Whether drama, horror, or comedy, these shared characteristics are present in nearly every "goth favorite," from music to comic strips.

Isolation is a major theme in goth films and literature, whether real or imagined. Characters in classic goth fiction tend to have their isolation forced on them by an outside world that does not understand or cannot accept them. Some modern writers and filmmakers have taken a more philosophical approach, examining how behaviors and lifestyle choices create a perceived sense of isolation that becomes a sort of self-fulfilling pattern for the tragic hero.

Intelligence and "hidden qualities" are also common characteristics for goth heroes. The hero might harbor hidden powers or may be faced with a secret past that dominates the character's psyche but also endows him or her with special gifts. Many goth heroes are portrayed as intelligent, often to the point that their intelligence allows them to recognize the faults, fallacies, and superficiality of the world around them (again returning to the all-important sense of isolation).

Setting is very important in goth stories, serving the role of a secondary character that either threatens or supports the protagonists. A threatening environment might be the outside world, depicted as bland, ugly, banal, and polished—everything that the character despises. A supporting environment might include any kind of strange and twisted alternate world, mirroring the inner life of the goth hero. From haunted houses to alternate dimensions, these otherworldly realms are depicted as places where the goths truly belong, rather than in the mundane world and daily drudgery of normal life.

Perhaps the most important quality is differentness. Dracula was a misunderstood, dangerous, and intelligent creature living in a gothic castle and preying on unsuspecting humans with sexy bloodsucking. Jack Skellington, leader of Halloweentown, was the only member of his community who dreamed of experiencing the pleasant joys of Christmas as a change from the endless daily Halloween festivities. These characters, separated by more than a century and cast in vastly different stories, had many traits in common. Most important, they were unique—singularities in a world where most everyone seemed to follow the same tune.

It is perhaps this quality of differentness that speaks most to members of the subculture. Mainstream society is where the majority of people spend their lives. The music they listen to, the books they read, the activities and fashion they enjoy, all fall into a broad category, blending countless traditions and influences but churning out a culture that favors conformity and "sameness."

Most goths are people who, for whatever reason, realize that this mainstream life is not for them. They feel different and often isolated but believe that they also have unique qualities to offer, if not those generally appreciated by the public at large. In the twisted worlds of fiction, the art student can become an action hero and the recluse can become the protagonist. Goth culture is itself a mix of reality and fiction and therefore, literature and film fill a very important niche, providing emotional release, inspiration, and an often comforting escape from the judgmental realities of the everyday world.

Notes

1. Andrew Smith, *Gothic Literature* (Edinburgh: Edinburgh University Press, 2007), 1–40.
2. Markman Ellis, *The History of Gothic Fiction* (Edinburgh: Edinburgh University Press, 2000), 1–30.
3. Smith, *Gothic Literature*, 70–78.
4. Joseph Laycock, *Vampires Today: The Truth about Modern Vampirism* (Ann Arbor: University of Michigan Press, 2009), 150–60.
5. Jason K. Friedman, "'Ah am witness to its authenticity': Gothic Style in Postmodern Southern Writing," in *Goth: Undead Subculture*, ed. Lauren M. E. Goodlad and Michael Bibby, 199–201 (Durham, NC: Duke University Press, 2007).
6. Deborah Wilson Overstreet, *Not Your Mother's Vampire: Vampires in Young Adult Fiction* (Lanham, MD: Scarecrow Press, 2006), 12, 21, 70–74.
7. Nancy Kilpatrick, *The Goth Bible: A Compendium for the Darkly Inclined* (New York: St. Martin's Griffin, 2004), 167.
8. Ibid., 168–70.
9. Personal interviews conducted November 2009–April 2010.
10. Daniel Bernardi, *Star Trek and History: Race-ing towards a White Future* (New Brunswick, NJ: Rutgers University Press, 1998), 2–10.
11. Daniel Pinchbeck and Ken Jordan, *Toward 2012: Perspectives on the Next Age* (New York: Penguin Group, 2008), 228–34.
12. Rick Worland, *The Horror Film: An Introduction* (Hoboken, NJ: Wiley-Blackwell, 2007), 1.
13. Alan Larson Williams, *Republic of Images: A History of French Filmmaking* (Cambridge, MA: Harvard University Press, 1992), 34–36.
14. Worland, *The Horror Film*, 40–45.
15. Ibid., 47–50.
16. Ibid., 157.
17. Ibid., 60.
18. Karen Kelly and Evelyn McDonnell, *Stars Don't Stand Still in the Sky: Music and Myth* (New York: Routledge, 1999), 50–53.
19. Jessica Burstein, "Material Distinctions: A Conversation with Valerie Steele," in Goodlad and Bibby, *Goth*, 270–73.
20. Tim Burton, *Burton on Burton* (New York: Macmillan, 2006), 5–7.
21. Catherine Spooner, *Fashioning Gothic Bodies* (Manchester, UK: Manchester University Press, 2004), 180–85.
22. Ibid., 183–84.
23. Ibid., 184–85.

CHAPTER
FIVE
| The Community
of Goth

Goth culture is a complex phenomenon that exists on many levels simultaneously. From one standpoint, goth can be viewed as a category of consumer products (including music, literature, clothing, and accessories) and the people who purchase and use these goods. Goth culture is also a community, or more precisely a set of communities, separated at times by thousands of miles and language barriers but still connected by shared interests and adherence to an aesthetic sensibility that remains recognizable across borders and cultural lines.

The notion of a goth community differs depending on region and on which part of the subculture is under scrutiny. In some cities and towns, goths gather only at music venues and in circles of close friends, while in other places, goths organize huge gatherings that blend music, fashion, and other goth commodities with the potential for networking and interaction. There is also a virtual goth community conducted through the Internet, which ties together small local scenes and individuals from around the world, increasing the distribution and reach of goth-themed media and also creating a transnational sense of belonging for many goths in the culture at large.

We Built This City . . . on Goth Rock

National and local goth communities grew out of the groups of fans, critics, organizers, promoters, producers, and other peripheral parties that gathered at goth concerts and at venues that supported goth music. Similarly, the members of many of the first goth bands met each other in communities organized around punk rock bands in Britain and the United States.

Clubs hosting concerts by Joy Division, for instance, might also display flyers from other bands with complementary sounds. Joy Division fans would then go to some of these concerts where they would see others they recognized from previous concerts. Along the way, members would share information about shops where they purchased clothes and recordings of new bands. Promoters and band members themselves would visit the concerts too, spreading the word about upcoming events. Within a short time, regulars were arriving at all the local clubs catering to this new sound, and a community was born.

In the 1980s, music magazines like *Sounds*, *NME*, and *Melody Maker* began reporting on the emerging goth bands in England. It was in the pages of these magazines and in radio interviews that goth received its name and that the word about the music spread. Photos of early proto-goths even appeared in style and culture magazines, helping to spread the popularity of the look as well as the sound.[1]

Around 1982/83, Mick Mercer, one of the most influential goth supporters of all time, became editor of the music magazine *Zig Zag* and began to steer the magazine's content toward the emerging goth sound. Mercer went on to write books focused on goth music and on the community as a whole, becoming one of the major forces in bringing together the fans of this music and making them feel that they were part of something larger—a movement and a community.[2]

In the 1980s, Mercer and other independent music writers reported on goth music as if it were the most innovative thing coming out of the international music scene. Within a few years, the edginess was lost and many mainstream music critics seemed to feel that goth was no longer worth the interest. Reviews of new goth bands even bashed the music, calling it derivative and overly melancholy, while other new bands were simply ignored. When the mainstream press lost interest, it strengthened the community as diehard fans felt they were part of something more exclusive, dismissed by a shallow popular market and therefore all the more exciting and innovative.

This is where the "fanzines" came into play. Fanzines are low-budget magazines, generally produced and published independently by fans who want to share their interests with the larger community. The fanzine phenomenon emerged long before goth music, as similar self-published literature was ubiquitous during the psychedelic rock movement of the 1960s and the punk rock scene of the late 1970s.[3]

While some fanzines were dedicated to single bands or artists, others attempted to cover the scene as a whole, or to at least cover all goth events in a certain area. Producing articles about new music, fashion, and other community developments, fanzines helped to organize local fans and also kept local communities informed about gothy developments in other areas. While most fanzines had a limited readership, some became very popular outside their home range and were sometimes distributed through mail-order to other cities or even countries.

Mail-order music and fashion supply companies also played an important role in propping up this emerging translocal community. Before there were stores in shopping malls selling goth music and clothing, items were available through mail-order companies, which advertised in the backs of magazines and fanzines and through flyers distributed at concert venues. Specialty mail-order companies allowed bands unable to attract mainstream recording contracts to reach potential fans on a national or even international level.[4]

Online Communities and Net Goths

Toward the end of the 1980s, people were only beginning to grasp the potential for using Internet communication as an avenue for networking and social interaction. Within a decade, social networking sites and Internet interest groups would be the standard for translocal organization, but in the early 1990s these were just beginning to form. Goth culture has always had its share of computer savvy participants, so it is perhaps not surprising that the first goth newsgroup, "alt.gothic," first appeared in these early days of social networking.

Alt.gothic got started thanks to a request from newsgroup user Laura Lemay, who wanted a place where she and fellow goths could discuss music, fashion, community organization, and other issues. Alt.gothic officially went online on November 01, 1991, and the organization's charter, from alt.config, was posted by a gentleman known as Eldritch the Thrillseeker. The charter explicitly stated that the discussion group was dedicated to discussions about the goth subculture as well as things "mournful" and "dark."

On the 3rd of November a poster asked if the band Fields of Nephilim was goth. The following day the first "What is goth?" question was posted. Over the years, the questions "What is goth?" and "Is this thing goth?" have remained two of the most popular discussion topics for members of the virtual community.

The initial posters to alt.gothic are now sometimes referred to as the "Great Old Ones," in typical goth faux mystical speak. In addition to Laura Lemay and Eldritch, there was Hirez, GothPat, Klaatu, and Count Von Sexbat. These posters started the wheels turning with intelligent discussions and promoted the newsgroup through word of mouth to others in need of some community.[5]

Simon Brind, otherwise known as Count Von Sexbat, became one of the culture's most eloquent diplomats, and he was, in the lingo of current posters, GAF (Goth As F**k). Sexbat contributed to the completion of the first FAQ for the alt.gothic community, a list of answers to frequent questions such as "What is goth?" and "How do I post on alt.gothic?" Sexbat remained a major figure in the subculture for nearly two decades, eventually becoming a well-known DJ who hosts traditional goth and eighties music nights at some of the most goth-centric gatherings in the world.

Another dedicated early poster on alt.gothic was journalist Mick Mercer, whose articles in the 1980s had already made him a well-known figure in goth circles. Mercer contributed to discussions on a variety of topics and also became one of the biggest proponents of organization, hoping to create a more cohesive musical movement out of what had become a rather scattered community.

Mercer promoted his community-oriented views on alt.gothic and also wrote a series of books, starting with *Gothic Rock Black Book* (1988),

GOTH BIBLES

Several publications have used the name "goth bible," though none of them so far have been about goth spirituality. Mick Mercer decided to use the name "goth bible" for his series of subcultural directories, collecting contact information for bands, artists, and organizations around the world that might interest goths.

collecting resources of interest to goths from around the world. Mercer did not believe that he was dealing with a simple musical genre and its related aesthetic; he believed strongly that he was involved in a social/cultural revolution.[6]

Alt.gothic became very popular, and within a couple of years the sheer number of posts and discussions was turning some goths off to the experience, especially as American goths began dominating the group. In response, a group of British goths started uk.people.gothic in June of 1995 as a place for people to discuss music, fashion, and other events of primary interest to goths in the United Kingdom.[7]

Over the years, the alt.gothic community developed its own traditions and its own language. A poster calling himself Erithromycin, or "Erith," created a thread called "se7en," which encouraged posters to post seven item lists of things on their minds at that moment. The original se7en thread became one of the most popular and longest continuing threads on the site.[8] The FAQ pages and other discussion threads on alt.gothic have served through the years to help many curious visitors understand more about goth culture, goth likes and dislikes, and the difference between goth culture and other groups like "Emo," described on the FAQ as "goth minus the f***ing."

Some of the goths who frequented alt.gothic began calling themselves and each other "usenet goths," which was later shortened to "net.goth." While this appellation originally referred only to goths using alt.gothic, some now use the name to refer to any goth with an "online presence." Some dedicated net.goths distributed stickers, T-shirts, and other stuff with "Net Goth" logos and slogans on them, intended primarily for those who participate in alt.gothic.

Goth Gatherings

As anyone who has been a dedicated user of online networking will attest, there comes a point when friends who meet online begin pondering the possibility of meeting face-to-face. For dedicated members of the alt.gothic community, this led to Convergence, an annual party attended by net.goths and friends and featuring music, a market for goth-friendly products, and other varieties of fun.

The first Convergence was held in 1995, after a discussion thread in which users proposed and then voted on potential locations. Lawrence, Kansas, was initially proposed for its geographic centrality, but Chicago was eventually chosen as the final spot. The party took place on June 23–24, 1995, and featured concerts by well-known goth bands including Lestat, Seraphim Gothique, Lycia, and Mephisto Waltz.[9] In 1996, Convergence was held in Boston, featuring Sunshine Blind, Switchblade Symphony, and others. Attendees also took group tours of Boston cemeteries, enjoyed a buffet dinner, and had the opportunity to participate in a goth fashion show.[10]

By 2009, Convergence had reached its 15th year, after stops in New Orleans, Las Vegas, San Francisco, and even Montreal, Canada. Convergence XV took place from July 17 to 20 in Long Beach, California, aboard the *Queen Mary* cruise ship. There was only one live band scheduled, The Last Dance, but the party also featured nine DJs spinning traditional goth, darkwave, a variety of EBM, and other goth-friendly electronica. In addition, there was the now traditional fashion show and a variety of group dining events on the schedule.[11]

The net.goths were not the only ones to come up with the idea of staging regular social events for goths outside their immediate area. In Philadelphia, local organizer Patrick Rodgers holds a quarterly party known as "Dracula's Ball," billed as "the largest event of its kind in America."[12] Rogers, often dressed in long hair, a black trench coat, and vampire fangs, says that the crowd is diverse, containing a mix of goths, vampire enthusiasts, clubbers, fetish enthusiasts, and people just looking for a good party.[13]

Dracula's Ball attracts as many as 2,000 attendees, primarily from East Coast cities but with a smaller number coming from far-flung cities and even international locations. In 2010, Dracula's Ball celebrated its 50th anniversary with live concerts from Ego Likeness

GOTH CRUISE

The annual goth cruise began as an idea at the fourth annual Convergence in Las Vegas and resulted in 64 goths taking a Carnival cruise ship to Cozumel. The cruise inspired documentarian Jeanie Finlay to produce a film about the phenomenon, asking, "How the hell did goths end up choosing to go on a cruise?"

and Bela Norte, in addition to a variety of DJs. Rogers encourages vampire-goth participation and many of the attendees do not disappoint, arriving dressed in some of the most convincing vampire costumes seen off the silver screen.

For goths in the United Kingdom, Whitby Gothic Weekend (WGW) is one of the most popular events. The gathering is held in Whitby, a town mentioned in Bram Stoker's famous vampire novel *Dracula*. At the first Whitby gathering of 1994, the attending goths (then a small group of friends) stayed at the Elsinore Hotel and caroused in the attached pub. Within a few years, the crowd outgrew the Elsinore and spread to nearby hotels and pubs. The Whitby community has embraced the phenomenon, having already become familiar with visitors attracted by the town's prominence in vampire lore.

In 2010, the WGW attracted between 1,000 and 2,000 visitors to the sleepy seaside town. The main events are the concerts held at the Whitby Spa Pavilion, featuring goth and related genres. In addition, there is the Bizarre Bazaar, an outdoor market where vendors sell clothing, jewelry, music, and hundreds of other gothy products. For some independent vendors of goth goods, the Bazaar is essential to building a customer base. Those who encounter interesting products at WGW spread the word to other potential shoppers and allow vendors to build catalogs of online customers to supplement their local sales.

The mecca of goth gatherings is Wave-Gotik-Treffen (WGT), an annual party held in Leipzig, Germany that attracts crowds of more than 30,000. WGT features more than 100 live bands and a dozens of DJs spinning a diverse complement of dark sounds, from traditional goth to neo folk and Japanese visual kei. Vendors from across Europe congregate to sell music, clothing, and other goods to the assembled

Participants of the wave gothic festival pose in Leipzig, eastern Germany, on May 22, 2010. (AP Photo/Sebastian Willnow)

masses, and the gathering also attracts vendors and artists representing other subgroups and cultures from creative anachronism to polka. The festival is held on the holiday of Whitsun (or Pentecost), approximately seven weeks after Easter.

The German appetite for goth and partying goes beyond what one festival can accommodate, so it is not surprising that the Germans also started the second-largest goth festival in the world, M'era Luna, an annual dark music festival that attracts as many as 20,000 attendees. Like WGT, the M'era Luna festival caters to a variety of subcultures, from strict goth to medieval rock and industrial. In addition to live concerts, M'era Luna's festivities include a lecture circuit, poetry readings, book signings, and myriad other events.

With both the largest and the second-largest goth gatherings in the world, Germany has become not only the capital of goth music but also the global center of the goth community. While the German festivals may be difficult for American fans to attend, they are one-of-a-kind experiences, with music and social events found nowhere else in the world. In Germany, goth has found a home where it is not only celebrated but embraced and, while some U.S. goths might wish to keep their communities more exclusive and underground, the German goth scene shows that goth can hit the big time without losing its authenticity.

To Commune or Not to Commune

The idea of a "goth community" does not appeal to all goths. Some goths have no real interest in meeting and greeting other goths, and are instead only interested in the music, the attitude, and the lifestyle. Even goths who enjoy the social aspect of gothdom might not want to participate in anything as large as M'era Luna or Dracula's Ball, preferring the intimacy and immediacy of a local environment.

Though it is not universally embraced within gothdom, the larger goth community provides important benefits to the subculture as a whole. The international community allows for the dissemination of music, fashion, and other products and also provides opportunities for those seeking to make their living in the subcultural economy. A goth living in a small midwestern town, for instance, will have a difficult time making a living selling only to local customers. The translocal communities of goths and associated interests provide a way for these vendors to increase their customer base. A single appearance at one of the festival markets might allow a local vendor to build sufficient online clients to quit his or her day job.

One of the drawbacks to organizing a translocal community is that the resulting entity will no doubt lose some of the exclusivity that exists in smaller communities. In a gathering of 20,000 or more, vastly different attitudes and personalities will be represented and clashes are inevitable. The feeling of such an event is much different than among a crowd of familiar regulars at a local goth bar in their hometown. Whether or not they utilize the larger community, goth gatherings, both physical and virtual, constitute a potential resource for goths around the world and an opportunity to make new friends, gain new experiences, and expand their horizons, real and otherwise.

Notes

1. Paul Hodkinson, *Goth: Identity, Style and Subculture* (New York: Berg, 2002), 111–15.
2. Nancy Kilpatrick, *The Goth Bible: A Compendium for the Darkly Inclined* (New York: St. Martin's Griffin, 2004), 112–13.
3. Chris Atton, *Alternative Media* (Thousand Oaks, CA: Sage, 2002), 110–20.
4. Andy Bennett and Richard A. Petersen, *Music Scenes: Local, Translocal and Virtual* (Nashville, TN: Vanderbilt University Press, 2004), 137–40.
5. Alt.gothic, http://www.altgothic.com/wiki/index.php/Alt.gothic.
6. Ian Peddie, *The Resisting Muse: Popular Music and Social Protest* (Surrey, UK: Ashgate, 2006), 179–85.
7. UK.people.gothic FAQ, http://www.countb.areti.co.uk/upgfaq/faq.html#1.
8. Erithromycin, http://www.altgothic.com/wiki/index.php/Erithromycin.
9. Convergence 1, http://www.altgothic.com/wiki/index.php/C1.
10. Convergence 2, http://www.altgothic.com/wiki/index.php/C2.
11. Convergence XV, http://www.altgothic.com/wiki/index.php/C15.
12. Kilpatrick, *The Goth Bible*, 106–8.
13. Ibid., 106.

CHAPTER SIX

The Perennial Gothic

A Culture of Difference

In its broadest definition, a subculture can be described as a group that is different from the mainstream, but not all subcultures have the same motivations for diverging from the status quo. Some subcultures are formed passively, such as those revolving around a sport or pastime. Gamblers, for instance, are members of a subculture in which gambling and the conventions that surround it play an important role in their personal and social lives. Gamblers do not choose to gamble, however, *because* most people do *not* gamble.

By contrast, some subcultures place greater emphasis on being *intentionally* different from the mainstream. These groups are united in their rejection of any number of things (like beliefs, conventions, clothing, music, etc.) that are embraced by the mainstream. Punks, for instance, may wear their hair colored in bright, bold colors to make a statement of individuality. If it catches on and everyone on their block starts choosing bright-colored hair, they might opt for a different direction, choosing a style that again sets them apart and makes them feel unique, different, and unusual.

Being individual and unconventional may be part of what drives some subcultures, but those who join in the social aspects of a subculture are generally also seeking to connect with others whose views and tastes are similar to their own. Inevitably, as soon as individuals decide to form a group, a new hierarchy begins to develop, with its own conventions, norms, and standards of behavior.

It is seemingly ironic that all groups, even those based on rejecting the conformity of the masses, end up developing their own cultural guidelines that lead to, in effect, a kind of similarity through anti-conformity. This happens for a variety of reasons, not the least of which is the need to recognize each other as insiders. The need for recognition plays a role in determining a culture's clothing choices and other outward symbols of membership. Also, in order to form bonds, members must be able to understand one another, and this drives the development of group-specific language and modes of interpersonal behavior. In other words, members of subcultures dress and act similarly to facilitate the development of the group, and that group, in turn, develops limits and boundaries determining who may gain membership and how members are expected to behave.

It seems that all cultures are doomed to some level of conformity. However, belonging to a group can provide a multitude of benefits, ranging from the pragmatic to the intangible, and to most people these benefits are worth some sacrifice in individuality. In addition, conforming to subcultural standards is far different from conforming to mainstream society. Goths, for instance, endeavor to create an environment free from sexism, racism, and homophobia—prejudices that are far more prevalent in the mainstream and tend to push individuals toward the periphery of society.[1]

As discussed earlier, goths tend to venerate outcasts and those belonging to marginalized social groups. This is partially due to the fact that many goths report feeling like outcasts in their own youth, divided from the mainstream by their unconventional tastes, attitudes, and desires. Some of these goths may have therefore gravitated toward a community in which being an outcast was the desirable thing. Members of ethnic minorities and those practicing some form of alternative sexuality sometimes enjoy an advantage within goth

GOTHS OF COLOR

More than 90 percent of American goths are white, but "goths of color" are increasing in number. In addition to African, Latino, and Asian goths, other ethnicities are also represented in some areas. Arizona goth band Black Fire, for instance, is a true rarity, headed by goths from the Navajo Nation.

subculture, held in higher esteem because of their "double outcast" status.

While the subculture incorporates many ethnicities, most goths are of European descent, or, as they are typically called, "white people." One of the lasting effects of European colonization is that there are now populations of white-skinned and brown-skinned people around the world with little connection to their original racial heritage. In the United States, many white families are a blend of European ancestry, without substantial connection to any culture in particular. Some sociologists have suggested that this lack of cultural connection has inspired mixed European descendants in the United States to identify with alternative groups, perhaps deepening the need for subculture.

In some ways, goth culture provides this context for its members by suggesting connections to an ancient (and largely idealized) European tradition. Groups of goths who dress in Victorian clothing, for instance, and even adopt some aspects of social behavior from the period, may feel that they are taking part in a type of alternative cultural lineage. In effect, the goths have created a tribe of fictionalized culture, within which any individual, regardless of his or her own background, can become part of a virtually timeless tradition. The symbolism adopted by goths provides one example of this mix of European heritage at work within the subculture. Ancient Celtic and Druidic symbols, for instance, are popular with goths, though often displayed in modern expressions, from jewelry and printed T-shirts to tattoos and piercings.[2]

It might even be argued that, in some cases, goth has become a type of fantasy ethnicity, superimposed on the physical features of the individual. Whether one's skin is brown or white, the black dress, makeup, and other aspects of the goth look take precedence, creating a sense of belonging that is beyond ethnic origin.[3] In these ways, goth culture can potentially provide for its members a substitute for biological family, history, cultural tradition, and even race.

As these arguments suggest, there is far more to being goth than simply wanting to be different. There are many ways to set oneself apart from the mainstream, but those who choose to be goth also must have an interest in a highly uncommon and specific set of tastes and desires. The gothic aesthetic is derived from the dark side of human nature, from the dangers that threaten our lives and the social and spiritual response to fear, death, and loss. As such, goth culture is part of a cross-cultural tradition, reaching perhaps to the very foundations of human existence.

The Gothic Canon

A 15-year-old would-be poet writing deeply wrought sentences about pain and loneliness probably does not feel much like he is part of a literary tradition, but his clumsy verse mimics the more dexterous pen of Edgar Allan Poe and hundreds of other poets who explored this bleak landscape. Gothic literature was first recognized as a distinct genre of fiction in the 1700s, but these writers too were following in the tradition of others who had long before penned poems and fables about death and life.[4]

Just as the gothic writers encouraged readers to confront their fears through stories about monsters, murderers, and supernatural forces, in ancient cultures oral stories were used to evoke the same emotions and the same thoughtful examinations of life itself. In fact, every aspect of goth culture can be seen as a modern interpretation of the ancient concept of investigating life through death.[5]

The fear of death has been such a dominant force in human culture that there is virtually no aspect of behavior or society that is divorced from its influence. Spiritual concepts regarding an imagined afterlife have likewise left their mark on every facet of existence. Dramatic goth rockers and teenagers dressed like vampires may seem to have little in common with these far more serious questions about the nature of life and the universe, but there are inroads between the two.

In many historical cultures, fear of death and the supernatural inspired ceremonies and rituals designed to prolong life and protect the living from whatever mysterious dangers lie in wait in the unknown. Over decades and centuries, these ceremonies began taking the form of celebrations, like Dia de los Muertos (Day of the Dead) in Mexico and the tradition of Halloween in the United States and Europe. Celebrations of this kind effectively combine reverence for death with a sort of tongue-in-cheek frivolity.

This is one of the roles that goths play in modern society. Their daily Halloween-esque behaviors transform serious and disturbing issues into something more lighthearted. Playing on these fears may be a psychological coping mechanism, symbolically taking control over factors of life that are nearly always out of one's control.

There is a serious side to goth culture as well. The intimate depression expressed through the lyricism of a goth rocker is in many ways similar to the confessional poetry and prose of writers stretching back to antiquity. Again, it is another way to face a painful and disturbing issue—by embracing and exploring it rather than trying to hide from the anguish. For some, this method of addressing loss, pain, and loneliness may be preferable to and more satisfying than the tack taken by those who choose the "forget about it and think about something else" approach.

In both their serious and more playful sides, goths are not alone in history, but are presenting the world with a modern rendition—complete with electric guitar, transgendered love, and electronic beats—of a very old artistic tradition. Not everyone identifies with this type of expression, but it has always been part of the human response to fear, pain, and the unknown.

Goth culture has consciously taken ownership over this creative canon, from gothic novels to the symbolism and rituals of earlier cultures. All those things that are sometimes called "gothic" are now part of "goth," and the goths have added to this body of work. While any individual may be able to recognize the appeal of a vampire film or the exhilaration of a scary movie, the goths make these things part of their daily lives and indulge more completely in this morbid take on the world.

The Goth Gene

As of this writing, there are teenagers across America who are encoun-tering goth culture for the first time. Somewhere in the middle-class suburbs of Saint Louis, Missouri, for instance, there is probably some young girl who is just now listening to a recently downloaded album from a band like Lacuna Coil. In the confines of her bedroom, she lets the music fill her head and finds something there, something in the sound that seems to speak directly to her. Perhaps she cannot explain exactly what it is or why she feels drawn to it, but when she listens, it is like looking in a mirror and seeing herself as the artist.

When asked about how they first came to find the subculture, many goths report that they were "always drawn to dark imagery and sounds." It is not uncommon for goths to describe their attraction to the goth aesthetic as "natural" or "instinctual." This brings about an interesting question: are people born goth?

Each year, the subculture's membership is bolstered by the addition of a new host of teenagers and preteens attending their first all-ages dark music nights or joining online discussion groups. Some of these newcomers are attracted to the culture because they are experiencing the familiar feelings of loneliness and isolation that are part and parcel of being a teenager. This "teen angst," as it is often described, has been attributed to a variety of potential causes, from the social difficulties of balancing increasingly adult desires with one's expected teenage roles, to nervous system activity in the teenage brain.[6]

Goth is often dismissed in the mainstream as a culture of teenagers, whose innate depressive impulses steer them toward dark imagery and depressing music. This is a misconception, as the

---

ELECTRO ANGST

In 2002, scientists at San Diego State University found that teenagers experience a rapid increase in electrochemical activity during puberty. This increased neuron activity in the brain makes it difficult to process information, leading to feelings of emotional and social instability.

subculture is actually driven by people who have outgrown their angst and still find themselves drawn to the dark aesthetic. Many may have taken their first steps toward goth along a path of adolescent inquiry, but found, in the subculture and its accompanying artistic creations, something much more substantial than a youthful phase.[7]

Artist Troy X. Musto, who markets his paintings under the name Lovely Corpse, found goth music and culture as a teenager. In his own description, his connection with "gothic" imagery was fueled by a Catholic upbringing and the interest he took in the religious iconography he was exposed to as a child. From an early diet of aggressive rock and metal, Musto's musical tastes gradually changed and he became drawn to the more cerebral and atmospheric music of the 1980s goth bands.

Musto was never a dedicated follower of the subculture, but his interest in goth music and in certain elements of the overall aesthetic remained a strong part of his personality well into adulthood. In his late 30s, Musto still preferred to dress in black T-shirts (one of his favorites being a well-worn shirt bearing a skull-and-crossbones logo), he still listened to Joy Division and The Cure, and his art continued to exhibit the gothic stamp, though blended with quasi-religious imagery, graphic artistry, and a variety of other influences.

Some of those who discover the goth aesthetic in their youth will eventually lose interest as their feelings and tastes change. Within the subculture, there are names like "gloom cookie" and "mall goth" used to describe would-be goth teenagers whose interest is thought to be motivated by an adolescent search for identity or by their chaotic teenage mind state. There are many others, however, like Troy Musto, for whom this dark aesthetic becomes a lifelong interest. These goths follow the same tradition as the eighteenth-century writers who penned the classics of gothic literature, and the nineteenth-century clothing designers whose Victorian fashions made funeral garb chic. The gothic aesthetic is, and has always been, one with both youth and adult appeal.[8]

Science and psychology may someday identify a phenomenon in which a person can be "wired" to respond to the goth aesthetic. Whether due to some Freudian syndrome or even potentially to genetic predisposition, there seems to be a certain portion of the population who simply have a much stronger and more emotional response to the underlying aesthetic within goth music, literature, fashion, and other forms of expression. This is not meant to suggest that some babies display a preference for black diapers or vampire-fang pacifiers, but rather that some people may be born with a physiological complement that makes them more responsive to certain cues. In any case, it seems that many of those who eventually become goth developed their aesthetic preferences at an early age, long before they realized that there were others out there with similar tastes and desires.

A common misconception about goth culture is that goths "recruit" members to their ranks. Researcher Michael Du Plessis, who has written about identity in goth culture, believes that actual recruitment is rare in this subculture. Du Plessis describes goth as a culture of "auto-recruitment," in which those who eventually "join" the culture gravitate toward the music and the social atmosphere on their own, often investing significant time and effort before gaining acceptance from members of their local community.[9] For their part, goths frequently make it difficult for newcomers, sometimes ignoring unfamiliar attendees until they "prove" themselves through demonstrations of interest and dedication.[10]

Those who instinctually gravitate toward goth music or literature learn to "be goth" by participating in the culture, seeking out others who share their perspectives and attitudes. The fear that goths are out recruiting kids, while perhaps appealing to those wanting to claim that goth subculture is perverting America's youth, falls short of reality. Parents of teenagers who have begun dressing in black and listening to goth music will probably discover that their teenager has not been brainwashed by a cult, but rather that he or she is actively participating in the formation of a new persona, inspired and perhaps encouraged by those who share common attitudes and interests, but based primarily on cognizant aesthetic choices that just "feel right."

The Goth Will Rise Again

If "illuminator" Pierre Remiet had been born in the nineteenth century, rather than the fourteenth, he might have been a goth. The mysterious French illustrator, whose miniature drawings of funeral scenes, dead rising from their graves, skeletons, and murder scenes graced a number of medieval French books and manuscripts, was seemingly obsessed with death, creating a style that almost resembled modern comic book art.[11] Similarly, poet and writer Edgar Allan Poe (1809–49), whose work has been enthusiastically embraced by goths, would probably have fit in well at a goth club, finding the camaraderie of others whose idea of beauty included the bleak and macabre.

Perhaps if there is a "goth mind state," artists like Remiet and Poe had it, choosing as they did to dedicate much of their artistic energy toward works of morbid and disturbing beauty. Given the antiquity of this gothic expression and the fact that the aesthetic still has a strong (if very different) presence in modern society, it could be argued that there have always been goths. A medieval bard who found that he only really liked to sing funeral elegies, or an Egyptian weaver who preferred the look of black fabrics and images of Set, the God of Death, might have been the "goths" of their own ages, drawn to the allure of these darker expressions.

This line of inquiry is not intended to overshadow the unique nature of the modern goth subculture, which is an independent phenomenon with merit outside any past manifestations. The intention here is to suggest that there may always be some people, in any culture, who are not moved by mainstream tastes (at times even repelled by them) and who find that, for whatever reason, they are drawn to this alternative aesthetic. Those people will have the option to embrace and contribute to the canon of creative works made by others with similar leanings.

The appeal of writers like Poe and Byron and artists like Remiet stretches far beyond goth culture. Anyone who can enjoy the thrill of a frightening film or find something intriguing about the seductive power of a vampire can on some level *understand* the appeal of this aesthetic, whether or not they share it. The longevity and international appeal of goth culture demonstrate that there are thousands around the world for whom this aesthetic holds more appeal than can be satisfied by a single annual Halloween ball or the occasional horror film.

In looking at the evolution of goth music and fashion, it is possible to recognize several distinct, but interrelated, stages. In its genesis, goth was a genre of post-punk rock, and the subculture that emerged from this environment was centered around gatherings at concert venues. Goth is now basically in its "third wave," wherein electronic music and virtual communities organized through the Internet have become dominant expressions of the subculture. Are these very different manifestations part of the same culture, or are we actually viewing separate subcultural manifestations of the goth aesthetic?

Goth has evolved in concert with Internet communication and the dawn of a new age of globalized information. On one hand, this has meant that goths can now find each other across a much larger audience, with goths in Ohio able to follow the newest music and literature from goths in Japan. On the other hand, the rapidity of cultural exchange has meant that goth is now threatened by a much larger audience of potential usurpers. The recent spate of vampire films aimed at teen audiences is a fitting example, showing how the masses can co-opt a genre that was once quite powerful within the subculture and transform it into something watered down for mainstream consumption.

In the face of this new world, goth culture may respond by evolving more creatively and rapidly than before, staying one step ahead of the trends. For a time, goths might abandon the vampires, waiting until the fad has died down before donning their fangs once again. In the interim, new and ever more imaginative takes on the genre will develop. In a culture dominated by artists, connected across international lines, and taking part in an ancient tradition of expression, there will always be room for new innovations and a new type of goth to stand in contrast to the mainstream.

It is perhaps the fact that goths have embraced the historical manifestations of their aesthetic that has allowed the culture to endure even as other subcultures emerge and wash away in rapid succession. Goths are a culture of both the present and the past and, in some ways, an expression of the fragile mortality that is always part of the human psyche. Edgar Allan Poe probably never imagined his poetry set to electric guitar, and, similarly, the goths of today can scarcely imagine how their kindred folk several decades from now will express their lifestyle and ideals. However, as culture will always be divided into dark and light expressions, complementary and opposing takes on every aspect of existence, we can imagine that there will always be artists, writers, and musicians who take up the torch, providing the world with a reflection of its strange and unsettling beauty.

Notes

1. Lauren M. E. Goodlad and Michael Bibby, "Introduction," in *Goth: Undead Subculture*, ed. Lauren M. E. Goodlad and Michael Bibby, 20–30 (Durham, NC: Duke University Press, 2007).
2. Interview with Michael Du Plessis, May 17, 2010.
3. Goodlad and Bibby, *Goth*, 371.
4. Andrew Smith, *Gothic Literature* (Edinburgh: Edinburgh University Press, 2007), 20–28.
5. Ibid., 160–61.
6. Duncan Graham-Rowe, "Teen Angst Rooted in Busy Brain," *New Scientist* (October 16, 2002), http://www.newscientist.com/article/dn2925-teen-angst-rooted-in-busy-brain.html (accessed July 2010).
7. Matthijs van de Port, *Authenticity* (London: LIT Verlag Munster, 2004), 90–102.
8. Ibid., 97.
9. Interview with Michael Du Plessis, May 17, 2010.
10. Paul Hodkinson, *Goth: Identity, Style and Subculture* (New York: Berg, 2002), 1–30.
11. Michael Camile, *Master of Death: The Lifeless Art of Pierre Remiet* (New Haven, CT: Yale University Press, 1996), 1–20.

Biographical Sketches

Music

Music is the central force in goth subculture, serving as a point of both unification and division. Goth musicians set the tone for the culture, demonstrating appropriate style and attitude and, through their lyrics, interviews, and other statements, also serve as spokespeople for the culture as a whole.

During the late 1980s and throughout the 1990s, hundreds of goth bands formed around the world, each contributing to the collective milieu and taking the culture in new directions. The artists listed here are "foundational" to the culture, representing the first innovative wave of musicians who inspired the emergence of the genre. This list constitutes an introduction to "early goth," but does not begin to touch on the vast variety of artists that followed in their footsteps.

The lives of many important goth artists are shrouded in mystery, not because there are any groundbreaking secrets involved, but because they have made a conscious choice to keep elements of their lives private. For instance, Sean Brennan, creator of music under the name London After Midnight, now places great emphasis on hiding the details of his family life and upbringing from the public eye after suffering what he describes as "persecution" for his lifestyle and the associations of his music. Similarly, many goth musicians, when asked about their lives and upbringing, give only vague answers.

Despite the often-intentional haze surrounding the lives of goth musicians, the details of their early lives often follow a similar pattern. Many goths were raised in suburban areas in middle- or upper-middle-class white families and many were "creative loners," interested in art, music, or other creative endeavors. Most goth musicians also fall into this mold, hailing from similar environments and often driven in their creative endeavors partially out of a rejection for the perceived superficiality and banality of the environments in which they were raised.

Whatever their backgrounds, the artists represented here and the artists who followed them took transformed their early inspirations into an original form of expression that resonated with thousands of people around the world. Goth culture today still contains the echoes of each of these artists and is a testament to the bizarre, sometimes absurd potential of those who dedicate their lives to creativity.

Steven "Abbo" Abbot

There is a good deal of debate about which bands belong in the pioneer goth band category, but many older goths would list Luton, UK–based band UK Decay among those early pioneers. The front man of the band, singer and guitarist Steven "Abbo" Abbot, has also been one of several musical people credited with naming the whole goth movement, when he stated in a February 1981 issue of *Sounds* magazine that UK Decay was into a "gothic" thing.[1]

Abbot was raised in Luton, England, a town of 200,000 inhabitants located in Bedfordshire. Luton is approximately 30 miles from London along the M1 motorway, and therefore enjoys spillover in terms of movies, music, and other diversions. Abbot was exposed to a variety of music in his youth and quickly took to playing instruments.

Abbot learned to play guitar in high school and began writing his own lyrics. In 1978 he joined The Resistors, a Luton punk outfit that also included vocalist Paul Wilson, Martyn "Segovia" Smith on bass guitar, and Steve Harle on drums.[2] When Paul Wilson left the group in the winter of 1978, Smith, Harle, and Abbot remained together, taking the name UK Decay and releasing a two-song seven-inch single record in conjunction with another Luton band, Pneumania.

From the start, Abbot and his band mates were interested in more than making music. Along with the local label Plastic Records they created Luton's first punk music boutique and clothing shop, Matrix, freeing local fans from the difficulty of driving to London every time they wanted a record. The shop was located in a four-story building on John Street, with the first floor dedicated to sales and a basement rehearsal space where UK Decay readied material for their first release. The shop lasted for only a couple of years, closing in 1981 after the basement flooded during a heavy rain.

Abbot functioned as the band's guitarist and lead vocalist at first, but later asked guitarist Steven Spon, from the band Pneumania, to become UK Decay's lead guitarist. The four played well together, and they began playing live shows within a few weeks of Spon coming on board. The band's first show together was at the Luton Town Hall in 1980.

Early in 1980, UK Decay released a four-song extended play (EP) recording, containing the songs "Black Cat," "Disco Romance," "Middle of the Road Man," and "Message Distortion." The photos on the EP cover already showed the beginnings of the goth aesthetic. Abbot is wearing dark clothing and looks thin and somewhat lost in the shadows. The inside cover even featured a shot from the German vampire film *Nosferatu*. After the EP hit the independent record charts, a representative from Fresh Records offered the band a recording contract.

In September of 1980, UK Decay released their first seven-inch single "For My Country," which stayed on the independent charts for eight weeks, reaching number 13 at its peak. Around that same time, UK Decay left Luton and played a show with the band Bauhaus in Northampton. Driven by the success of the single, Fresh Records soon scheduled the band for a UK tour with American punk band the Dead Kennedys. After some lineup changes, they released their first full-length album, *For Madmen Only*, in October 1981.

It was in a 1981 interview with *Sounds* that Abbot described his band's music as a "gothic thing." Many music history buffs cite this as a defining moment, though Abbot has expressed his ambivalence at being known as the man who gave goth its name.

Fresh Records went under in early 1982 and everything recorded under the label was purchased by the newly formed Jungle Record. Abbot and his band mates scrambled to get sufficient funds together to purchase the rights to their recordings and started their own label, UK Decay Records. Internal strife overpowered their collective success and the band dissolved in 1982. During their short time together, UK Decay played more than 400 shows, and their energy in live performances became the stuff of goth legend for the next generation.

In 1988, Abbot formed Big Cat Records Ltd., a record label with clients ranging from punk and indie rock to jazz and classical music. He later joined Bedlam Artist Management, a company representing artists in the recording and performing businesses. When the company was purchased by Virgin Group in 1997 and became known as V2 Records, Abbot worked in the company's international division, helping to set up satellite operations throughout North America. In 2000, Abbot was named head of A&R for V2.[3] During this time, he helped to find and sign such artists as Moby, the White Stripes, and the RZA.[4]

Notes

1. Peter Scathe, "An Early History of Goth," http://www.scathe.demon.co.uk/histgoth.htm (accessed June 28, 2010).
2. Martin Charles Strong, *The Great Indie Discography* (Edinburgh: Canongate Press), 2003.
3. "Executive Turntable," *Billboard*, February 26, 2000, 8.
4. UK Decay official Web site, http://www.ukdecay.co.uk/ (accessed June 28, 2010).

David Bowie (Born 1947)

Rock icon David Bowie has long been celebrated for his ability to change. While some artists develop a sound that is characteristic of a certain time and/or place, Bowie has reinvented both himself and his music in concert with the ebb and flow of the times. *Rolling Stone* magazine called him a "consummate musical chameleon,"[1] while biographer Jesse Jarnow described him as an "intellectual shapeshifter."[2] Bowie's relevance to goth culture began in the mid-1970s as he crafted a musical persona that blended rock, theatrics, and his unique lyricism to create what is now known as "glam rock."

Bowie was born David Robert Jones in Brixton, a southern borough of London.[3] He showed an early affinity for music and, with his friend George Underwood, participated in numerous amateur bands, playing jazz and cover songs.[4]

It was a falling-out with Underwood that gave Bowie one of his most recognizable features. When he was 14, Bowie thwarted Underwood's relationship with a young woman in a contest for her affections. Enraged, Underwood belted his best mate, and his fingernail caught Bowie's left eye, damaging the muscles of the eye. Bowie's permanently dilated left pupil added to his mystique as his face became familiar to fans. Before biographers explained the accident, fans created a host of potential explanations for the eye, ranging from a fight gone wrong on the London streets to the influence of extraterrestrials.[5]

By age 16, Bowie was a working musician with a number of bands to his credit, and he had completed his first studio recordings with his R&B group Davie Jones and the King Bees. Bowie also recorded with two of his other bands, the Manish Boys and Davie Jones and the Lower Third.[6]

Discouraged by limited success, he embarked on a solo career and, to distinguish himself from singer Davy Jones of The Monkees, he took the name David Bowie, borrowing from Colonel James "Jim" Bowie who perished at the Battle of the Alamo and who famously killed an enemy with a large knife, now known as a "Bowie knife." Most biographers agree that David Bowie chose the name because of the knife, rather than the Kentuckian folk hero.[7]

In 1967, Bowie studied theater and mime with Lindsay Kemp, who had been a student of perhaps the only person to hold the title "famous mime," Marcel Marceau.[8] Bowie was a mediocre mime, and miming was, as it is now, the taciturn stepchild of the theater. He formed a dance/mime/theatrical troupe called Feathers, which lasted for only a year or so before he moved on to louder endeavors.[9]

Armed with a hodgepodge of experience, the young Bowie was inspired by the imminent *Apollo 11* moon landing and wrote the album *Space Oddity* in 1969. Bowie's song about lost astronaut Major Tom was withheld until the real-life *Apollo* astronauts were safely back on terra firma and then was released by the BBC, becoming a number 5 hit and Bowie's first commercial success. The follow-up album reached number 16 on the British pop charts.[10]

Bowie was openly bisexual, a fact that would later earn him his label as a "sexual revolutionary." In 1969, Bowie was having an affair with Calvin Mark Lee of Mercury Records, who was also bisexual and was also having an affair with Angie Barnett, a cover girl, musician, and artist.[11] Bowie and Barnett met through Lee and married in 1970, a marriage that produced Bowie's first son, Duncan Zowie Haywood Jones, and ended with a somewhat spiteful divorce in 1980. Lee would thereafter be remembered as the man who was simultaneously sleeping with both Bowie and Bowie's first wife.[12] As his fame grew, Bowie stirred controversy when he admitted he was gay in an interview for the music magazine *Melody Maker*.[13]

In December of 1971, Bowie released the album *Hunky Dory*, often cited as the beginning of glam rock. He upped the ante the following year, with the creation of his alter ego Ziggy Stardust. Bowie based the character on a variety of influences including the Stardust Cowboy, a country musician with a popular stage act based on a space-faring cowboy.[14] Bowie *became* Ziggy in 1972, with his band now known as the Spiders from Mars. Their concerts soon involved all sorts of theatrics including multiple costume changes, miming, and other dramatic interludes. Ziggy gave Bowie a face for the media and a way to express the most dramatic elements of his persona. His 1972 album *The Rise and Fall of Ziggy and the Spiders from Mars* was the culmination of Bowie's rock experiment.

Bowie's glam period was tremendously influential on the goth generation. Those who formed foundational goth bands like Bauhaus often cite Ziggy as one of their early influences. Bowie's flair for drama, his dark, introspective lyricism, and his gender-transgressing androgyny became staples of the goth scene. In 1982, Bowie added another accomplishment to his list that would likely make him the envy of many modern goths; he portrayed a vampire in Tony Scott's fantasy horror film *The Hunger*.[15]

Throughout the late 1980s, Bowie's music was poppier, though his lyrics were often deeper and sharper than the average pop ballad. His 1983 album *Let's Dance* was his biggest commercial success, with chart-topping singles released internationally. Bowie also composed music for films including John Schlesinger's 1985 film *The Falcon and the Snowman*. In 1986, Bowie had a starring role as "Jareth the Goblin King" in Jim Henson's big-budget puppet fantasy *Labyrinth*.

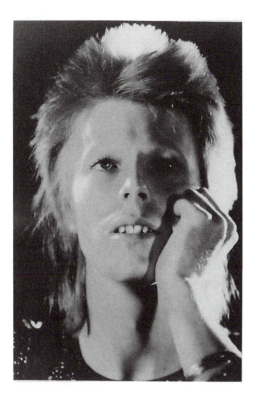

British glam rocker David Bowie is seen in 1973 during his Ziggy Stardust period. (AP Photo)

Over the next two decades, Bowie was always involved in some new project, whether musical, theatrical, or otherwise. None of his albums released during the 1990s captured the same critical or audience acclaim, but he still displayed an uncanny ability to produce music that did not sound dated. In 1992, Bowie married Somalian model Iman, and the two had a daughter, Alexandria Jones, born in 2000. While his catalog of work is profound, Bowie's legacy will also be about the bravery to express the fullness of one's personality through performance.

Notes

1. "David Bowie," 2009, http://www.Rollingstone.com (accessed September 2010).
2. Jesse Jarnow, "David Bowie," in *Icons of Rock: An Encyclopedia of the Legends Who Changed Music*, vol. 2, ed. Scott Schinder and Andy Schwartz, 481 (Westport, CT: Greenwood Press, 2008).

3. Marc Spitz, *Bowie: A Biography* (New York: Random House, 2009), 20–25.

4. Ibid., 35–40.

5. Ibid., 38–39.

6. Jarnow, "David Bowie," 482–83.

7. Nicholas Pegg, *The Complete David Bowie* (Richmond, Surrey, UK: Reynolds & Hearn, 2000).

8. Jarnow, "David Bowie," 486.

9. Ibid., 487.

10. Spitz, *Bowie*, 104–24.

11. Christopher Sandford, *Bowie: Loving the Alien* (New York: DaCapo Press, 1998), 55.

12. Jarnow, "David Bowie," 487.

13. Sandford, *Bowie*, 85.

14. Spitz, *Bowie*, 153.

15. Ibid., 315.

Ian Curtis (1956–80)

The post-punk band Joy Division lasted only three years before coming to a premature end with the suicide of lead singer Ian Curtis. Joy Division attracted an avid following and pioneered a different sound, creating atmosphere and ambience that stood out in an environment where raw anger and angst ruled the musical milieu. Joy Division is now recognized as a forerunner of the goth genre, and the band's small collection of recordings are still a staple in goth music libraries.

Ian Curtis was born in July 1956 in Manchester, and lived with his parents and sister in Macclesfield, a town outside Cheshire, England, for most of his life. Biographies of Curtis describe him as a sensitive and somewhat distant teenager.[1] He was inspired by music from an early age, including the Velvet Underground and punk/glam rock pioneers like David Bowie and Iggy Pop.[2] Later he also became a fan of punk rock bands like the Sex Pistols. He had a deep fascination with musicians and stars who died young, which is not uncommon for teenagers, but has come to be seen in a different light since Curtis's suicide placed him among the same ranks.[3]

Curtis met his wife, Deborah Woodruffe, in Macclesfield and they married in 1975. The couple had a daughter, Natalie, in 1979, and remained married until Curtis's death.[4] Curtis worked for the Training Services Division, a branch of the local government charged with finding jobs for the unemployed. He remained with the government until

1979, when the success of his band convinced him to pursue music full-time.[5]

Curtis met his future Joy Division band mates after answering an ad in the newspaper looking for a lead singer.[6] In May 1977, the band (then called Warsaw after a David Bowie song) played their first concert at the Electric Circus.[7] While passionate, it was clear they were not masters of their instruments, and reviews were mixed. *New Music Express* writer Paul Morley saw potential in the young band, writing that they had an "elusive spark of dissimilarity."[8]

In early January 1978, the band changed its name to Joy Division, a name taken from the term used by German Nazi officers to refer to groups of woman prisoners kept as prostitutes.[9] In April, they gave the finale performance at the Chiswick Challenge, a multiband concert sponsored by Stiff Records. Producer/TV host Tony Wilson and band manager Rob Gretton were captivated by their performance and Wilson invited the band to appear on his Granada TV program, while Gretton took over as their manager.

Joy Division recorded a live session with music icon John Peel in February of 1979 and soon recorded a full-length release called *Unknown Pleasures*, which received favorable reviews. Though he was a new father, Curtis had a troubled personal life. For several months Curtis had been having an affair with a young Hungarian artist, a fact that threatened his relationship with his wife. In addition, Curtis' drinking and drug use were beginning to take a heavy toll on his health and mental state.

Though punk had been on its feet for only a few years, it was already dying, and bands like Joy Division and The Cure were pointing the way to the future. The Cure's music would form a pillar of what would later be called "new wave," while Joy Division created a more mellow, dark, introspective sound. Partial credit must go to producer Martin Hannett, who used synthesizers and distortion to add to the lonely, distant ambience.[10] Their success continued into early 1980 with the release of their second full-length album, *Closer*.

In 1980, the band was preparing to leave for a North American tour set to begin in May, but it was a tour that would never come to be. On May 18th, with his wife spending the night away with her parents, Curtis hanged himself in his kitchen. During his final hours,

Curtis wrote a long and painful letter to his wife, lamenting his inability to end his affair, even to save his marriage.[11]

Writers Karen Kelly and Evelyn McDonnell write of Curtis in *Stars Don't Stand Still in the Sky*, "Joy Division started the movement from the energy and anger of 1976's punk revolution to the self-pity that would characterize the new wave of the eighties."[12] Everything about Curtis, from his personal demons to his tortured lyricism and deep, doleful voice, stood out from everything around him. Kelly and McDonnell said of his voice, "It said nothing if not that Ian Curtis was an ordinary man in extraordinary pain."[13]

Despite their limited output, Joy Division inspired a passionate following that persisted into the twenty-first century. The 2007 documentary *Control* explored the life of Curtis, Joy Division, and their global impact. As goth began to emerge, Curtis's style and poetry became symbolic of the impulses, aesthetics, and overall "feel" that differentiated this new movement from the mainstream. Kelly and McDonnell posit that Curtis's death was an important moment in the formation of goth: "They needed a folk hero like Ian Curtis to die for them," they write, "so they wouldn't have to discover for themselves that death had no sting."[14]

Notes

1. Mick Middles and Lindsay Reade, *Torn Apart: The Life of Ian Curtis* (London: Omnibus Press, 2009).
2. Deborah Curtis, *Touching from a Distance: Ian Curtis & Joy Division* (London: Faber & Faber, 2005), 10–26.
3. Ibid.
4. Ibid.
5. Phillipe Carly, "Joy Division Central," http://www.joydiv.org (accessed July 28, 2010).
6. Curtis, *Touching from a Distance*, 2.
7. Middles and Reade, *Torn Apart*.
8. Curtis, *Touching from a Distance*, 3.
9. Karen Kelly and Evelyn McDonnell, *Stars Don't Stand Still in the Sky: Music and Myth* (New York: Routledge, 1999), 50–53.
10. Ibid., 52.
11. Ibid., 5.
12. Ibid., 52.

13. Ibid.
14. Ibid.

Peter Murphy (Born 1957)

Musician Peter Murphy has been called the "Godfather of Goth"[1] and the "Goth King."[2] As the lead singer for the British post-punk band Bauhaus, Murphy's abysmal lyricism and baritone delivery helped to define the goth sound, while his thin, teetering-on-the-edge-of-collapse appearance was imitated by hundreds of young proto-goth boys around the world.

Murphy was born in Northhampton, England, and spent most of his youth in Wellingborough, a commuter village close to London. Like many who gravitated toward the punk scene, Murphy was a fan of David Bowie, T-Rex, and the other glam rock bands. He was much more into this type of theatrical rock than the fiery and crude punk sound that was emerging in the 1970s.[3]

In 1978, Murphy joined the Northhampton glam rock band The Craze. With Murphy on board, they headed in a darker direction, a gloomy take on glam pop that would define a new genre.[4] The band was renamed Bauhaus 1919, a reference to the German architectural school that opened in 1919 and utilized a modern, minimalist approach to design (though they dropped the "1919" part when they recorded their first album).[5] Among the songs on the demo was a track entitled "Bela Lugosi's Dead," which became the band's debut single when it was released by Small Wonder Records in 1979.

Of all the songs recorded by Bauhaus, their debut single is the most famous and the most iconic. The song became a true goth anthem, inspired both by Murphy's dark poetry and by band mate Daniel Ash's love for vampire imagery. The song also solidified the connection between goth and vampires, one that would continue to be reinforced through art, music, and literature.

Bauhaus released their debut album *In the Flat Field* in 1980 to critical acclaim. They followed with a second album, *Mask*, in late 1981 and a third, *The Sky's Gone Out*, the following year. Perhaps the biggest year for the band was 1983, but it was also their last year together. That year, the band released a cover version of David Bowie's hit "Ziggy Stardust," which became their biggest single.[6]

Murphy and the band were also asked to appear in the 1983 feature film *The Hunger*, which starred David Bowie as (of course) a vampire. Murphy and the band performed "Bela Lugosi's Dead" over the opening credits of the film, with the camera focusing largely on Murphy. As Michael Du Plessis writes in his essay " 'Goth Damage' and Melancholia," "The film puts glam-rock icon Bowie face to face with Goth icon Murphy by way of offering two distinct but equally androgynous gender styles that confront each other in a dizzying clash of fakeness—or realness."[7]

Murphy's fame in light of their appearance in *The Hunger* began to drive a wedge between the band members. Adding to this separation, Murphy suffered a bout of pneumonia that left him unable to contribute fully to the fourth album, *Burning from the Inside*.[8]

During Bauhaus's four years together, the band created the mold for goth music. Murphy's somber poetry and lifeless delivery combined with the band's purposefully undead aesthetic. They fed on the theme of death and decay, occasionally performing dressed in vampire regalia or rising from coffins. Every aspect of the band formed a part of what would later be known as the traditional goth aesthetic.

When Bauhaus broke up, Ash and the other band mates went on to form Love and Rockets, a successful rock band that released a number of well respected albums between 1985 and 2003. Murphy went on to engage in a variety of projects, releasing his first solo album, *Should the World Fail to Fall Apart*, in 1986, with a follow-up in 1988 and another in 1990. Murphy's solo efforts displayed a different musical sensibility, with greater diversity of musical influences and a softer overall tone.[9]

In 1992, Murphy moved to Turkey with his wife, Beyhan, a Turkish dancer and artistic director, when she was asked to serve as artistic director for a new modern dance company. There he began to explore Middle Eastern musical styles, traces of which can be found in much of his later music.[10]

In 2006, Murphy joined the former members of Bauhaus for a reunion tour, and produced a new album *Go Away White*, which contained elements of Murphy's solo music, Bauhaus's older material, and a spattering of Love and Rockets. Personal differences between the band mates brought an end to the promotional tour before it started and Murphy returned to solo recording.

Over more than three decades, Murphy redefined himself and his music in many ways. Though he has remained a consummate experimenter and musical innovator, his legacy has burrowed deepest at the roots, where he helped to define a sound that became a genre.

Notes

1. Manny Theiner, "Music Preview: Bauhaus Frontman Peter Murphy Tours with Solo Retrospective," *Pittsburgh Post-Gazette*, June 19, 2008.
2. Christian Logan Wright, "The Metamorphosis of Peter Murphy," *Spin*, November 1988, 24.
3. Ian Shirley, *Bauhaus: Dark Entries* (London: SAF, 2009), 12–32.
4. Nancy Kilpatrick, *The Goth Bible: A Compendium for the Darkly Inclined* (New York: St. Martin's Griffin, 2004), 80.
5. Shirley, *Bauhaus*, 26–29.
6. Ibid., 50–80.
7. Michael Du Plessis, Michael, " 'Goth Damage' and Melancholia," in *Goth: Undead Subculture*, ed. Lauren M. E. Goodlad and Michael Bibby, 163 (Durham, NC: Duke University Press, 2007).
8. Shirley, *Bauhaus*, 80–102.
9. Dave Thompson, *Alternative Rock* (Milwaukee, WI: Hal Leonard, 2000), 511–12.
10. Theiner, "Music Preview."

Roger Alan "Rozz Williams" Painter (1963–98)

Rozz Williams was the singer for some of the best known early goth bands in the United States, including Christian Death and Shadow Project. Before his suicide in 1998, Williams was becoming known as a pioneer, creating a harder, violent take on the basic sound that came to be called "deathrock."[1]

Williams was born in Pomona, California, in 1963, the youngest of four siblings. Like many in the future goth scene, Williams was inspired by the sounds of David Bowie, T-Rex, and the New York Dolls and became a regular at punk rock concerts. By age 16, Williams had developed into a talented vocalist and a passable guitarist.

In 1979, Williams and guitarist John "Jay" Albert formed Christian Death, joined by bassist James McGearty and drummer George Belanger.[2] The name was a twist on the name of fashion designer

Christian Dior.[3] The band's first performance was at Hong Kong Café in Los Angeles, accompanied by fellow dark rockers 45 Grave.

Personality clashes between the band members caused Christian Death to break up in 1981. Williams's next project was an experimental blend of performance and music that he called *Premature Ejaculation*, a collaboration with Los Angeles performance artist Ron Athey. Athey and Williams entered what Athey described in an obituary printed by the *Los Angeles Times* in 1998 as "a love affair that lasted three years."[4]

Premature Ejaculation's performances were bizarre collections of sounds and noises accompanied by poetry written by Athey and Williams. Athey reported that the two became heavily involved with heroin and other drugs, in an effort to "fuel their creativity." Athey would often mutilate himself onstage as part of the performance, and once ate and regurgitated a road-killed cat, presumably more for art than flavor. "We were true punk romantics," writes Athey, "he pierced my nipple, I tattooed his name on my wrist and slashed his wrists open with a straight razor."[5]

Williams reconstituted Christian Death in 1983/84 with guitarist Valor Kand, keyboardist Gitane Demone, bassist Constance Smith, and drummer David Glass. This was the most popular incarnation of Christian Death, and the band's popularity quickly expanded beyond the Los Angeles scene. It was largely with this, the third incarnation of Christian Death, that Williams began pioneering the more aggressive direction that was later called "death rock." The band was commercially successful but Williams left in 1985, while some of the remaining members kept the act alive and continued recording throughout the 1990s.

Williams's next band, Shadow Project, a duo with vocalist and guitarist Eva Ortiz, better known as "Eva O,"[6] has been called "metal," "goth rock," and even "glam rock." During more than a decade of recording and touring, they created a unique, sinister, and captivating sound. In addition, Eva O and Williams found they had chemistry beyond the recording studio, and were married in 1987. Shadow Project stopped recording in 1993, as Eva O left to pursue a solo project. Williams started another project, called Daucus Karota, with which he recorded an EP album in 1994.

In his later recordings, some reviews noted an emotional complexity not seen in some of his earlier works. Fans could only theorize as to how

Williams would have further developed as a musician, as he hung himself in his Los Angeles apartment on April Fools' Day, 1998. A memorial service was held later that month at the El Rey Theater, attended by friends and a cross section of the dark-music scene.

Williams's suicide was brought on by a depression that had plagued him throughout his life. Some friends have suggested that his increasing alcohol consumption also played a role in his worsening depression. "This was the life of an artist," wrote Athey in his *LA Weekly* eulogy, "a true Romantic who sacrificed normality, health and happiness for the sake of vision, and a man overcome and destroyed by the demons he lived with: a tragedy."[7]

Notes

1. Gavin Baddeley, *Goth Chic* (Medford, NJ: Plexus, 2002).
2. Rozz Williams, http://www.rozzwilliams.com (accessed March 23, 2010).
3. Baddeley, *Goth Chic*.
4. Ron Athey, "Rozz Williams 1963–1998," *LA Weekly*, April 8, 1998.
5. Ibid.
6. Annie Layne, "Goth Pioneer Rozz Williams Hangs Himself," *Rolling Stone*, April 9, 1998.
7. Athey, "Rozz Williams, 1963–1998."

Susan "Siouxsie Sioux" Ballion (Born 1957)

Singer and songwriter Susan Ballion, better known as "Siouxsie Sioux," has the honor of being the first "goth moll." Siouxsie's dark and outrageous fashion and her moody lyricism established a new archetype for the female musician and for female fashion. Though only her earlier work is generally acknowledged as gothesque, her influence over the genre is unquestionable, especially in defining the look for the gothic woman.

Siouxsie grew up in Kent, a suburb of southeast England. Her father died when she was 14 of complications arising from alcoholism. She entered her teens at a time when music was rapidly changing and innovative artists like Lou Reed and David Bowie were exploring a new chapter of rock. Soon she became a dedicated fan of punk rock as it spread through England.[1]

As Malcolm McLaren and Max Wooldridge write in their book *Rock 'N' Roll London*, "So many writers, artists, and musicians seem to hail from suburbia, for no other reason than there's so much to rebel against: the blandness, the boredom, the uniform conformity."[2] Siouxsie was one of a group of enthusiastic fans from the London suburb of Bromley who attended every Sex Pistols concert and stood out thanks to their enthusiasm and bizarre fashion.

The first time the whole group came together might have been at the Sex Pistols concert in January of 1976 at Bromley Technical High. Journalist Caroline Coon, writing in the magazine *Melody Maker*, was the first to refer to the group as the Bromley Contingent, and the name stuck.[3]

Siouxsie was among the most outrageous of the contingent, wearing outfits that were clearly meant to capture attention, including elements of fetish and BDSM (bondage, domination, sadism, and masochism) attire.[4] She wore makeup to highlight her pale skin, dark, dramatic eyeliner, and sometimes more experimental outfits, such as a dress that left her breasts exposed. It was a daring and original look.[5]

In September of 1976, Siouxsie formed an adhoc band for a performance at London's Club 100. Originally a jazz venue, the bar put together a punk showcase, featuring the Sex Pistols and a number of unknown acts in the same vein, including Siouxsie's newly formed band, the Banshees.[6]

Siouxsie had not written or learned any songs and instead recited poetry and the Lord's Prayer over more than 30 minutes of sound experimentation. While some reviewers described their first show as an unbearable cacophony of unrelated noises, Caroline Coon, one of the journalistic champions of punk, praised Siouxsie for innovation and style.[7]

Initially the Banshees consisted of Siouxsie, bassist Steven Severin, guitarist Marco Perroni, and drummer John Simon Ritchie. The lineup changed several times over the years, but they were one of the most enduring bands to emerge from the punk revolution, appearing in one form or another from 1976 to 2002.[8] In November of 1978, Polydor Records released the band's first album, *Scream*, hitting the top-10 singles charts in the United Kingdom.[9]

In 1979, they brought on drummer Peter "Budgie" Clarke, who was brought in as a temporary stand-in but became a permanent member. Clarke and Siouxsie's relationship became romantic in the 1980s and the pair married in 1991, remaining together until 2007.

The 1980 album *Kaleidoscope* was critically acclaimed and featured a more aggressive production style, with extensive use of synthesized sounds. The following year, the band released *Ju Ju*, another top-10 album, in which the band moved further from their punk roots toward a pseudo-gothic mélange.[10]

During the remainder of the 1980s, the Banshees spawned a couple of successful side projects, with Siouxsie and Budgie recording music under the name Creatures, while Severin went on to record with Robert Smith, a sometimes Banshees member who became famous for his own band, The Cure.[11] While they changed considerably, some of the band's 1990s albums, like *Rapture* (1996), were regarded by critics as their most interesting and polished releases.[12]

The Banshees disbanded in 1997 and reunited in 2002 for a reunion tour. After the 2002 re-breakup, Siouxsie took time away from music, finally returning with the release of a solo album, *Manta Ray*, in 2007, which achieved critical acclaim.

While Siouxsie's musical style changed considerably from her debut to her 2007 solo album, she never lost her edge. Critics often lacked appropriate descriptors for Siouxsie and the Banshees, largely because they were creating something new. For her own part, Siouxsie was a new kind of woman who became a role model for a new generation of women.

Notes

1. John Doran, "Siouxsie Sioux Interviewed: The Banshees and the BBC," *Quietus*, July 20, 2009.
2. Max Wooldridge and Malcom McLaren, *Rock 'N' Roll London* (New York: Macmillan, 2002).
3. Ibid.
4. Lauraine Leblanc, *Pretty in Punk: Girls' Gender Resistance in a Boys' Subculture* (New Brunswick, NJ: Rutgers University Press, 1999), 46.
5. Punk 77, "The Bromley Contingent," http://www.punk77.co.uk/groups/bromley2.htm (accessed June 28, 2010).
6. Karen Kelly and Evelyn McDonnell, *Stars Don't Stand Still in the Sky: Music and Myth* (New York: Routledge, 1999), 50.
7. Ibid., 50–53.

8. Mark Paytress, *Siouxsie and the Banshees* (London: Sanctuary Press, 2003).

9. Martin Charles Strong, *The Essential Rock Discography* (New York: Open City Books, 2006), 972–73.

10. Ibid., 973.

11. Ibid.

12. Ibid.

Storytellers

Goth is essentially a creative culture, built from music but also informed by fiction and fantasy. Literary scholars place the origins of gothic fiction and fantasy in the 1700s, but the genre's origins extend to the literary traditions of tribal societies long before modern literature was invented. The human fascination with the supernatural and interest in frightening stories probably had its origins in the oral traditions of ancient societies.

Over the centuries, writers, moviemakers, and other storytellers have re-created the gothic genre time and time again and, with each new version, helped to bring the timeless appeal of classic gothic themes into a modern perspective. Whereas early gothic novels were tales of horror, love, and loss, modern gothic storytellers place these archetypal struggles alongside contemporary issues including sexual ambiguity, psychosocial disorders, and the foreboding advance of mechanization. The modern gothic tale is informed as much by romanticism for the past as by the realities of modern life and the potential dystopian futures that stand before us.

The writers and filmmakers described here are four of the most successful storytellers in the genre, whose works have reached broad audiences from vastly different walks of life. What these storytellers have in common is the use of supernatural characters, settings, and symbolism to tell stories of human experience in captivating and intriguing ways. In addition, each of these artists has been embraced by the goth community and has played a role in creating the modern goth ethos.

From vampires and monsters to psychopaths and gods, these writers and filmmakers tell fantastic stories that provide escape from the everyday world while simultaneously directing focus back on reality itself, providing new ways of thinking about the experiences that bind cultures together.

Anne "Howard Allen" Rice (Born 1941)

Anne Rice is one of the foremost writers of gothic fiction, and though her work appeals most to those goths with "vampire fixations," her novels and film adaptations of her books have had a major influence on goth culture and fashion. Rice is also one of the most successful authors in America, having sold over 100 million books since publishing her first novel, *Interview with a Vampire*, in 1976.[1]

Rice was born Howard Allen O'Brien in New Orleans, Louisiana, the second of four daughters born to Katherine and Howard O'Brien. Named after her father, she took the name Anne on her first day of school, creating it on the spot when asked for her name by one of the school's nuns. Rice's mother died when she was 14 years old and, two years later, her father transferred in his job with the postal service to Richardson, Texas.[2]

Rice took an early interest in writing and met the man who would later become her husband, Stan Rice, in a journalism class at Richardson High School. Rice went on to study at Texas Woman's University in Denton, Texas, but kept in correspondence with Stan Rice, who proposed marriage in 1961, via telegram. After marriage, Rice and her husband relocated to San Francisco where both studied at San Francisco State University. Rice obtained a master's degree in creative writing while her husband published poetry and became an instructor for the university.[3]

In 1966, the couple had their first child, Michele, who was diagnosed with leukemia at an early age. Rice published short stories and essays and worked on a story that became her first novel, *Interview with a Vampire*, though it would not be published for another decade. Rice and her husband spent most of this period caring for their daughter, who passed away in 1972.[4]

Rice turned *Interview* into a novel the following year, but it took until 1976 to find a publisher. The book became a bestseller and Rice sold the film rights to Paramount Pictures, using the considerable windfall to fund extensive global travels. In 1978, Rice had her second child, Christopher, and transitioned into a life as a full-time novelist.

Many of Rice's novels focus on supernatural themes and characters, including most notably her collection of vampire protagonists. In interviews, Rice has explained that writing about vampires allowed her to explore her own views on complex subjects including the nature of religion and the threat of death.[5] Rice has said that one of her primary characters, the vampire Lestat, functions as a symbolic alter ego, representing the darker and more savage aspects of her personality.

By 1990, Rice was a best-selling author several times over and her books were popular on an international scale. She continued publishing books about vampires and supernatural themes, often utilizing characters connected to her first novel. In 1994, Rice's work hit the big screen with *Interview with a Vampire: The Vampire Chronicles*, starring Tom Cruise and Brad Pitt. The film was a success and had a major influence on local goth culture, inspiring an increase in both vampire and Victorian fashion for male goths.[6]

After a string of illnesses, Rice very publicly announced in 1998 her return to the Catholic faith, which she had abandoned at age 18. Rice stated that she did not agree with all of the Church's views, specifically their prohibitions on same-sex marriage and abortion, but had renewed faith and wished to dedicate her work to her higher power. In 2002, Rice's husband died soon after being diagnosed with brain cancer. Shortly after the publication of her 2005 novel, *Christ the Lord, Out of Egypt*, a biographical account of Jesus Christ during his childhood, Rice relocated to a private home in California near her son, Christopher, who, by this time, had become a successful fantasy novelist in his own right.

Since her return to religion, Rice's novels focus on spiritual and Christian themes but she continues to speak publicly about her earlier work. Rice is one of the only modern writers of gothic fiction whose work has reached extensive popular appeal. The underlying themes of sexual domination, dysfunction and violence in her early work made Rice's stories popular for literary evaluation. Though only her early novels and film adaptations have had a significant influence on goth culture, she stands as one of the most successful and inventive writers of modern gothic fiction, carrying on a century-old tradition of exploring the lines between life and death.

Notes

1. Chris Ayers, "The Conversation: Anne Rice," *Times Online*, November 7, 2009, http://entertainment.timesonline.co.uk/tol/arts_and_entertainment/books/fiction/article6905136.ece (accessed June 10, 2010).

2. Gary Hoppenstand and Ray Broadus Browne, *The Gothic World of Anne Rice* (Bowling Green, OH: Bowling Green University Popular Press, 1996), 16–17.

3. Ibid., 17–25.

4. Anne Rice, *Called Out of Darkness: A Spiritual Confession* (New York: Random House, 2008), 135–38.

5. Washington State University, "Anne Rice Biography," 2009, http://www.wsu.edu/~delahoyd/rice.bio.html (accessed June 10, 2010).

6. Hoppenstand and Browne, *The Gothic World*, 20–25.

Neil Gaiman (Born 1960)

Neil Gaiman is one of a small group of mainstream artists and writers whose work has been embraced by the goth community. From his long-running illustrated series of *Sandman* comics to his novels, Gaiman creates characters that resonate with goths, blending humor with his own affection for the dark and otherworldly. Gaiman has not limited himself to a single genre and has produced a formidable body of poetry, prose, journalism, comics, and novels, establishing himself as one of the most original storytellers alive today.

Gaiman was born in 1961 in Portchester, England, the first of three children. His middle-class family converted to Scientology when he was five, moving to East Grinstead, the center for the religion in Britain. Both his parents and sisters became deeply involved in the church and his parents later opened a chain of vitamin stores, selling supplements used in Scientology's Human Detoxification Program.[1]

Gaiman took an early interest in writing and tried for a time to publish short stories, unsuccessfully. He then set his sights on journalism as a career and found some success publishing in newspapers and magazines. Gaiman used journalism to meet with and interview some of the fantasy and sci-fi authors he admired, building a network of connections that would later help him to break into the industry. During this time, he also wrote and published a companion book to Douglas Adam's *Hitchhiker's Guide to the Galaxy* series and a few other collaborative book projects.[2]

Gaiman befriended comic book writer Alan Moore and learned from him how to craft a comic book story. He later submitted one of his stories to DC Comics and, though it was rejected, Karen Berger at DC began to hire Gaiman as a writer for various projects. In 1988, Gaiman published the first issue of his *Sandman* series, on ongoing

In this April 23, 2010, photo, best-selling author Neil Gaiman, 49, poses in his writing gazebo at his home in western Wisconsin. (AP Photo/Craig Lassig, File)

tale focusing on the experiences of a character who rules over the world of dreams.

Gaiman crafted the series in such a way that he was able to move from topic to topic, bending the ongoing narrative to include whatever subjects appealed to him at the moment. Dysfunctional families, transsexuals, displaced youth, and supernatural creatures have all appeared in the evolving story. One of the characters he created provided a new take on the classic mythological figure of Death, a guide who takes the recently deceased to their new existence. Gaiman avoided traditional imagery and instead portrayed the character as an attractive, intelligent, and compassionate young girl, a character that won many fans within the goth community and became one of the earliest portrayals of the now well-known "goth girl" archetype.[3]

Gaiman's first novel, *Good Omens*, a collaboration with famed science fiction author Terry Pratchet, was published in 1990 to much acclaim. He followed with the adult-themed 2001 novel, *American Gods*, which won a Hugo Award for fiction among a number of other accolades and became a bestselling book in both the United States and the United Kingdom. Gaiman built on the story with a sequel of sorts, *Anansi Boys* (2005), which was also well received. In 2008 Gaiman released a children's story, *The Graveyard Book*, with inspiration from Rudyard Kipling's masterpiece *The Jungle Book*.[4]

As Gaiman gained stature in the industry he also branched out into film and television, writing an episode of the fantasy, science-fiction series *Babylon 5* among a number of other projects. He also collaborated on writing the script for the film version of *Beowolf*, starring Angelina Jolie. Gaiman's writings have also been co-opted for theatrical release, including a 2009 animated film based on Gaiman's dark fable "Coraline."[5]

Gaiman built a thriving career on his imagination and become a storyteller on an international scale. In interviews, Gaiman is appreciative of his following among the goth community. He has said that he feels people are "born" with a tendency toward a certain way of looking at the world and that this innate feeling creates groups like goths— people sharing a similar way of seeing and feeling. Gaiman feels that he is one of those born with what he calls "a mind that wanders towards graveyards," and that this has allowed his writing to find an audience among kindred minds.[6]

Notes

1. Dana Goodyear, "Kid Goth," *The New Yorker*, January 25, 2010.
2. Michael McCarty, *Giants of the Genre: Interviews with Science Fiction, Fantasy, and Horror's Greatest Talents* (Rockville, MD: Wildside Press, 2003)," 46–48.
3. Rebecca Schraffenberger, "This Modern Goth (Explains Herself)," in *Goth: Undead Subculture*, ed. Lauren M. E. Goodlad and Michael Bibby, 125–26 (Durham, NC: Duke University Press, 2007).
4. Goodyear, "Kid Goth."
5. Neil Gaiman official Web site, "Biography," 2010, http://www.neilgaiman.com/p/About_Neil/Biography (accessed June 10, 2010).
6. Nancy Kilpatrick, *The Goth Bible: A Compendium for the Darkly Inclined* (New York: St. Martin's Griffin, 2004), 166.

Melissa Ann "Poppy Z." Brite (Born 1967)

Author Poppy Z. Brite is one of the most unique voices of gothic horror. With a thoroughly modern take on the genre, her work blends classic themes with substantive discussions of issues including race, gender, and sexuality.

Brite was born in New Orleans, Louisiana, and like fellow gothic novelist Anne Rice often used New Orleans and southern settings in her novels.[1] According to her own biography, Brite was a storyteller almost from birth, recording her early fables into a tape recorder before she could read or write.[2] By age 12, Brite was writing and submitting fiction to magazines, though it would be some years before anyone would publish her work. When she was 14, her parents divorced and Brite moved with her mother to Chapel Hill, North Carolina.

Her first successful submission was to the semiprofessional horror magazine *The Horror Show*, when she was 18. Over the next couple of years, she wrote and published additional stories in the magazine, which had a readership of around 10,000 at its peak.

Brite's contributions to *The Horror Show* came to the attention of Doug Winter at Walker & Company publishers, who were working on a new line of horror novels. Though she had recently enrolled at the University of Chapel Hill, North Carolina, Brite took the initiative, dropping her classes and beginning working on her first novel, *Lost Souls*.

Walker & Company abandoned the horror series after Brite's manuscript spent six months on the shelf. She moved to Athens, Georgia, around this time, a small town that she said heavily influenced the creation of her fictional North Carolina town, Missing Mile. In Athens, Brite met chef Christopher DeBarr, who later became her husband. "He was dancing wildly with his shirt off," Brite writes of the incident, "and tried to get me to take mine off too. I fell in love anyway."[3]

In 1991, *Lost Souls* was picked up by Dell Publishing and released the following year. Dell not only agreed to publish the book but also offered Brite a handsome contract for two additional novels. *Lost Souls* became an award-winning book and a best seller, though a segment of the horror audience was turned off by Brite's brutal descriptions of sexual violence. Brite's Lost Souls series involves vampires, but unlike in many traditional tales of gothic horror, her vampires are not cursed humans but rather a separate species living alongside and feeding on the human race.

Shortly after fulfilling the next part of her Dell contract with the publication of *Drawing Blood*, Brite and her husband moved to New Orleans. Her second novel received praise from both critics and fans, but when Brite turned in her third novel, *Exquisite Corpse*, Dell's editors returned the manuscript claiming that they could not publish it due to its "extreme content."

Exquisite Corpse was eventually published by Simon and Schuster and was a commercial success. While Brite's style nearly always involves weaving uncomfortable themes into her narratives, *Exquisite Corpse* took these themes to another level through her protagonist Andrew Compton, a homosexual serial killer, cannibal, and necrophiliac. The book was written in an almost journalistic manner, and Brite's characters brought such darkness to bear that some readers were turned off by the effort. Overall, however, the book received positive reviews and furthered Brite's reputation in the industry.

Shortly after, Brite was contacted by musician Courtney Love, a fan of her work, who asked Brite to pen an unofficial biography for her. The book was released in 1996, under the title *Courtney Love: The Real Story*. Though she could not officially authorize the work, Love gave Brite access to personal writings and other materials, in an effort to counter the number of other "biographies" that were published at that time.

After several years of publishing short fiction in various compilations, Brite moved into the dark-comedy genre, with a series of novels starting with the 2004 release *Liquor* from Three Rivers Press. She followed with several more books based on the same characters, a group of New Orleans locals working in the restaurant industry and navigating the perils and tragedies of their lives.

Brite's characters often deal with alternative sexuality and desires, subjects that are close to her own experience. Brite has openly admitted in interviews that she has grappled with gender identity, though never going as far as to brand herself as a lesbian or with one of the labels frequently used to describe those with alternative sexual interests. Brite feels that she has an innate emotional identification with homosexual males that has informed her work and helped her to bring her predominantly homosexual characters to life.[4]

Brite represents a very modern approach to the gothic aesthetic, facing not only the classic struggles of life, death, and spirituality, which are at the heart of the genre, but also the difficult and hazy areas between sexuality and gender, which are only beginning to become part of the American idea of identity. Through her *Lost Souls* series and further works, Brite has increased the reach of the gothic universe as she and her characters face monsters in both physical and psychological form.

Notes

1. Steven Jones, Kim Newman, and Peter Straub, *Horror: Another 100 Best Books* (New York: Carroll & Graf, 2005), 297–99.
2. Poppy Z. Brite official Web site, "Biography," 2009, http://www.poppyzbrite .com/bio.html (accessed June 15, 2010).
3. Ibid.
4. Poppy Z. Brite official Web site, "Rope," 1998, http://www.poppyzbrite .com/rope.html (accessed June 15, 2010).

Tim Burton (Born 1958)

Director Tim Burton has made a career out of bringing dark fantasy come alive on screen. Many of his characters and the general feel of his films capture part of the goth aesthetic and the general attitude about existence—the beauty of the twisted, the bizarre, and the shadowy corners of existence.

Burton was born in Burbank, California, which he later described in interviews as a "blank, unemotional environment."[1] Friends and relatives describe him as shy, withdrawn, and very artistically inclined. From an early diet of fantasy and horror films, Burton began creating crude films while only a teenager,[2] and in 1976, he attended the California Institute of the Arts, studying animation.[3]

In 1979, Burton took a job with Walt Disney's animation depart-ment. During this time, he produced his first solo films, including an adaptation of Mary Shelley's Frankenstein called *Frankenweenie*.[4] His films came to the attention of television actor Paul Reubens (better known as Pee-Wee Herman), who approached Burton to direct his 1985 hit film, *Pee-Wee's Big Adventure*.[5]

His next film was the 1988 dark comedy, *Beetlejuice*, a major hit starring Michael Keaton and Winona Ryder. Burton explored a subject that would come about in many of his later films—what happens when yuppie culture collides with the twisted. It was also in *Beetlejuice* that Burton first demonstrated his ability to create the unique and bizarrely beautiful environments that would come to characterize his work.

Beetlejuice was an effects hit on a relatively low budget, and studio executives decided they would see how Burton handled a blockbuster package, resulting in *Batman* (1990). The film was more mainstream, but still had Burton's unique vision.[6]

Between the first *Batman* and the sequel, *Batman Returns*, Burton created one of his most beloved films, the 1990 goth fairytale *Edward Scissorhands*. Considered by some to be his masterpiece, *Edward Scissorhands* emerged directly from Burton's mind. He wrote the story with coauthor Caroline Thompson, and was allowed complete creative freedom.[7]

Edward Scissorhands tells the story of a Frankenstein-like boy, played by Johnny Depp, created in a laboratory by a lonely scientist,

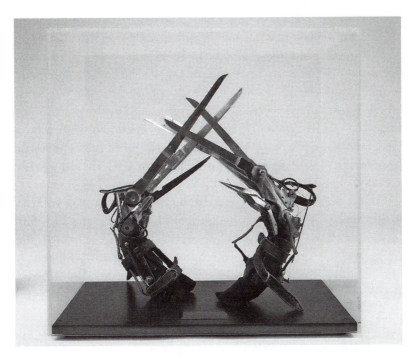

This photo released by Julien's Auctions shows a pair of the prop "scissorhand" gloves that Johnny Depp wore as he portrayed the title character in Tim Burton's Edward Scissorhands. *(AP Photo/Julien's Auctions, Shaan Kokin)*

played by Burton's childhood hero Vincent Price. The boy, stitched together from various bits and pieces, is left incomplete, with scissors instead of hands, when his maker dies. Thus deformed, he descends into the surreal, colorful suburbs that surround his gothic castle birthplace and attempts to find his way in an environment from which he has been isolated.

Edward Scissorhands has been called a "fable of goth otherness."[8] The symbolism runs deep, describing the adolescent search for identity through a boy whose very touch is a destructive force.[9] In an interview for MTV, Burton said of the film, "It was a symbol of those feelings you have as a teenager . . . and that dynamic of not touching and not being able to connect with people."[10]

Burton used a very goth aesthetic for his hero, fitting Depp with spiked black hair framing a sickly white face, contrasting with dark rings on the eyes and lips. He also dressed his hero in tattered black clothing with tight-fitting pants, all aspects of goth fashion as it emerged in the 1980s and early 1990s

Burton went on to write, but did not direct, the animated film *The Nightmare before Christmas* (1993), which also dealt with a hero who felt out of place and was searching for a new identity, and which also became a goth classic[11] along with his 1999 film, *Sleepy Hollow*, based on the ghost story by Washington Irving. Again, Burton cast the somewhat androgynous Depp as his hero, with a very goth look including period clothing in dark hues, dark spiked hair, and a pale complexion. His heroine, played by Christina Ricci, was equally gothesque in her period attire and pallid complexion.[12]

In the decade from 2000 to 2010, Burton added another six films to his catalog. Some were big-budget blockbusters, like the 2001 film version of *Planet of the Apes*, while others, like 2005 animated film *Corpse Bride*, were more in keeping with the shadowy fantasy of previous films. In 2010, Burton released his first 3D film, *Alice in Wonderland*, which was largely a family-friendly production, but still displayed Burton's characteristic stamp.

During this time, Burton's personal life developed as well. He started dating actress/model Lisa Marie in 1992, but the pair broke up in 2001, and Burton began seeing actress Helena Bonham Carter, who would appear in many of his future films. Burton and Carter had a son, Billy Ray, in 2003 and a daughter, Nell, in 2007.[13]

Over the course of his career, Burton has become one of the most unique and respected American directors. From coming-of-age fables to sinister horror and quirky biopics, Burton has developed a characteristic style that can adapt to many different genres. In interviews, Burton says that his own sense of "otherness" as a child and young adult still color the way he sees the world. The mainstream media linked Burton to the emerging goth subculture, and Burton, for his part, became a defender of the negative stereotypes lumped onto the goth kids by the media.[14]

Notes

1. Nancy Kilpatrick, *The Goth Bible: A Compendium for the Darkly Inclined* (New York: St. Martin's Griffin, 2004), 230.
2. Edwin Page, *Gothic Fantasy: The Films of Tim Burton* (London: Marion Boyars, 2007), 9–29.
3. "Tim Burton Biography," http://www.timburtoncollective.com (accessed March 2010).
4. Page, *Gothic Fantasy*, 14.
5. Ibid., 25–26.
6. Ibid., 55–60.
7. Ibid., 57–75.
8. Lauren M. E. Goodlad and Michael Bibby, "Introduction," in *Goth: Undead Subculture*, ed. Lauren M. E. Goodlad and Michael Bibby, 29 (Durham, NC: Duke University Press, 2007).
9. Goodlad, 30–32.
10. Larry Carroll, "Tim Burton Talks 'Nightmare,' Goth Kids, Frightening 'Friends' Episodes," Music Television News, October 23, 2006, http://www.mtv.com (accessed June 16, 2010).
11. Page, *Gothic Fantasy*, 131–40.
12. Ibid., 159.
13. "Tim Burton Biography."
14. Carroll, "Tim Burton Talks."

Glossary of Goth Slang

baby bat: A new recruit to the goth scene who does not yet have any knowledge of the local scene or culture.

corporate goth: Goth with a day job who dresses as a goth only after working hours.

cybergoth: Subgroup of goth culture marked by an interest in different genres of music, including futurepop, industrial, powernoise, and EBM. Most cybergoths also integrate elements of futuristic, computerized, or robotic influences in their clothing.

cybermuppet: Derogatory term used within the goth community for those who prefer the cybergoth scene.

dark cabaret: Genre blending Weimar-era cabaret and burlesque with darkwave and other goth influences.

darkwave: Name given to the traditional goth music of the early post-punk bands. Also used to refer to electronica goth music in the earlier manifestations.

destroyed (also, ravished): Term for being exhausted, intoxicated, or just plain worn-out, generally from too much gothy activity.

doom cookie: See gloom cookie

EBM: Type of dance music involving ominous sounding vocals or sound effects blended with beats similar to those in techno music.

elder goth: Goth of the older generation, especially one with knowledge of the goth scene in the 1970s or 1980s.

Elegant Gothic Lolita (EGL): Japanese style blending dark goth, "baby doll" fashion, and Victorian-inspired clothing.

EMO: Type of music usually involving emotional, confessional lyricism with moving instrumentation.

gloom cookie: A derogatory term used for disaffected young women who attempt to dress and act goth, but are generally considered outsiders and posers. Doom cookie is sometimes used for a male.

gothdom: Sarcastic term for goth culture and/or society.

gothed up: Word used to describe people who put on goth clothing, makeup, and other artifacts, especially for a night at the goth clubs.

gother-than-thou: Goth who believes him or herself to be more goth oriented than others. Also the name of a trivia game based on granting points for goth knowledge.

goth points: Tongue-in-cheek ratings system based on giving people points for choices seen as making the person more gothlike.

kindergoth: Young goth, generally under the age of 16, but most definitely preadult.

mall goth: Derogatory term used for goths who hang out in shopping malls and who get some of their goth accessories from mall stores like Hot Topic.

Mansonite: Person who listens to Marilyn Manson.

mopeygoth: Goth whose introspective tendencies often lead him or her to avoid the social aspects of the scene, as if he or she would rather be writing poetry of some sort.

mundanes: Term sometimes used to refer to those who are not part of the goth scene. Meant to convey the idea that the world outside the scene is less than interesting.

neo folk: Type of music largely developed in Germany that combines medieval and Renaissance influences with electronica and darkwave elements.

net.goth: Name used by some goths who participate in the alt.gothic discussion group, now generally used to refer to any goth with an online presence.

perkygoth: A goth who displays happy, even bouncy behavior, often dressing in lighter gothy style than other types of goths.

psychobilly: Type of music blending country, old time, bluegrass, and punk rock.

rivethead: Slang for a person involved in the industrial music scene.

romantigoth: Goth with a penchant for romanticism in both fashion and music taste.

spot the goth: Game played by some goths involving finding other goths within a certain environment. Can also be used to find the people who "would be" goths in other environments.

steampunk: Genre of fiction involving technological developments in an alternate world where steam and other alternative energies are employed.

trad goth: A person who adopts the clothing and enjoys the music of the original goth music and fashion. Sometimes used to refer to those who have been part of the scene since at least the mid- to late 1980s.

ubergoth: Someone who is considered very goth, more goth than others. Sometimes used in a derogatory way.

vampire goth: Goth who takes an interest in vampirism, whether manifested through personality, fashion, or interest in literature.

visual kei: Style of music developed in Japan, blending rock music with elaborate costumes and theatrical performances.

Primary Documents

The Scholarly Goth

Goth culture is diverse and has many unique facets, providing fertile ground for a variety of sociological research. A researcher could choose to study, for instance, the way that goth social networks form through focal points like clubs and concerts, or might instead focus on the formation and diversification of "virtual communities" through goth Web sites and discussion groups. Alternatively, researchers can delve into the development of gothic fashion or tackle complex, esoteric issues like the relationship between Japanese female goth fashion and body image.

In any case, goth subculture attracts a certain sub-sub-culture of researchers who are often attracted by the same aesthetic underlying goth as a whole. Compared to other music-based subcultures like urban hip-hop or punk rock, goths are relatively well educated, literate, and have a penchant for introspective self-expression, making them ideal for sociological evaluations. A large number of those who research goths either were part of the culture themselves at some point or at least have an affinity for either the music or the style.

Goth Researchers

Researchers Lauren M. E. Goodlad, Michael Bibby, and Michael Du Plessis were all contributors to the excellent scholarly volume *Goth: Undead Subculture* (2007). Professor Michael Bibby, from Shippensburg University, approached goth research through his interest in the 1980s Factory Records label and bands like Joy Division. Associate Professor Lauren Goodlad, of the University of Illinois, approaches goth culture through a personal interest in Victorian literature and culture and the work of modern gothic writers like Poppy Z. Brite. Professor Michael Du Plessis, from the University of Southern California, approaches goth culture through an interest in the formation of subcultural identity.

Interview with Michael Bibby, Lauren Goodlad, and Michael Du Plessis

MI: How would you describe goth culture to someone with no experience?

Bibby: Goth is a subcultural style that revels in the morbid, funereal, haunted, antiquated, melancholic, and darker sides of civilization; unlike death-metal or industrial music subcultures, though, goth tends to be nonaggressive and more masochistic—more about the romance and sublime pleasures of a death-haunted night-world.

Goodlad: I think I'd ask them to read the introduction to my book! Failing that, I'd see it as a youth culture/subculture that builds off of gothic rock music, whose participants tend to cultivate strong interest in aesthetics borrowed from various gothic forms in literature, art, fashion, and so forth.

Du Plessis: Like other post-World War II youth subcultures, goth, as a subculture based on music and very distinctive dress, makes and marks *distinction* in a mass culture. It places emphasis on sadness and melancholy and other "dark" kinds of emotions and affect and it looks back to aspects of 18th and 19th century Romanticism, Victorianism, and the Gothic as mode and genre in high culture (literature, painting, design). At points it overlaps with other subcultural forms like cyberpunk, steampunk, and emo. It depends on a strong sense of alienation and difference, which in turn produces a distinction between insiders and outsiders. Like other "spectacular" subcultures (that is, subcultures that draw attention to themselves through their visual marking of difference, such as punk or hip-hop), goth depends on the marking of difference from a "mainstream" that may or may not be entirely imaginary. At the same time, as with other youth subcultures after World War II, goth exists in an inescapable relation to a marketplace of mass-produced goods to which it has a simultaneously antagonistic and dependent relation. In other words, goth tries to create its difference precisely in and through commodities ("looks" and "lifestyles"), while claiming to challenge the dominance of identities by commodities (the "lifestyles" on the mainstream marketplace).

MI: What makes goth subculture interesting from a research standpoint?

Goodlad: I think it would have to be the perennialness of the subculture: thus, undead subculture. I should add that I don't know that the academy as such is more interested in goth than in other spectacular and youth subcultures. But for those who are, the perennial aspect of it doubtless constitutes its appeal and perhaps also the eclecticism. Then, too, the fact that goths tend to be so literate (which makes them very good subjects for literary critics).

Du Plessis: One of the issues in sociology/ethnography has been the constriction of the in-group, and in order to study this group it must be distinct in some way. [The goths] marked themselves more and more visibly, signaling their detachment from the outside. In terms of constructing a visible group, goth has done this and is therefore valuable to the study of group formation.

Bibby: It's an unusually enduring fringe subcultural style that resists assimilation into the mainstream—it's a scene that inspires a wide variety of cultural responses.

MI: Is music the central element to goth culture?

Bibby: Yes, music is the unifying theme by far—the music is what inspired the fashion, body imagery, etc. No one would claim, for example, that Johnny Cash is goth—he might have goth elements to his style ("the Man in Black"), but his music is so obviously NOT goth that it's definitive. A dark style doesn't make one goth, in other words— and although Joy Division never wore clothes or posed themselves in style that could be seen as goth, the band's music is cited by almost every goth as fundamental. Again, it's not the fashion or image that determines its "goth-ness" but the music. Judging from the various sub-cultural online communications (listservs, forums, blogs, etc.), goths always seem to self-identify first by their musical tastes.

Goodlad: I think at one point it was, but it no longer is. It would be hard to be a goth and not like goth music—or at least some of it. But I suspect that most goths have very eclectic tastes in music—and probably always have.

Du Plessis: Yes, with the caution that music is a part of a network of goth which crucially includes fashion, style, attitude, and "lifestyle." Music in goth can take its cues from the field of literature (Poe, for example) or film (classic horror, such as London After Midnight, a silent Lon Chaney film from 1927 that also gives its name to a goth band). In the significance of a particular musical sound (here, the dominance of minor keys and very particular rhythms and vocaliza-tions) goth is more like other youth subcultures of the past—punk in its 1970s form, or mods in the 1960s, or rockers in the 1950s.

MI: How would you describe the overall goth fashion aesthetic?

Bibby: A goth look really develops, I think, by turning a DIY "post-punk" art-school attitude towards glam fashion. Even Siouxsie Sioux's and Bauhaus' styles in 1979 self-consciously harked back to Bowie and glam.

Du Plessis: The aesthetic is of the impractical. The appeal is in the total dedication and purity [of the style] compared to other styles. It is still pure, still almost authentic in style. When goth style started emerging it was seen almost as a carnival, or a cartoon opposed to the "real" of punk. Now, it seems the more real. Also, the sense of the past is important, the sense of self-creation. In Los Angeles, there is a lot of Victorian influence and even trying to live as Victorians. There is a sense of creating an alternate lifestyle, of reading about and imagining a sort of distant world. Craftiness and a kind of DIY aesthetic thing. Ultimately it may be about finding control in an out-of-control world. Creating an environment in which death and apocalypse are in your control.

MI: What are your thoughts about the significance of moviemakers like Tim Burton to goth culture?

Bibby: Burton succeeds in mainstreaming goth because he comes to it as an insider of the subculture and often stays true to its aesthetic values (esp. early Burton). Most mainstream representations fail to hit the mark, though, because they try to mimic subcultural style from the outside—and because goth tends to mortify mainstream culture, to unsettle it. Mainstream, commercial culture almost always gets its wrong, stumbles in its attempts to commodify goth.

MI: What about the significance of Hot Topics chain stores to goth culture?

Du Plessis: More so even than Tim Burton, the Hot Topics brand has served as a kind of test for the mainstreaming of a mall-friendly version of goth. It seems telling that right now Hot Topics is primarily selling *Twilight* merchandise. Like *Twilight*, Hot Topics is now such a dilution of goth that it's become something else entirely.

Bibby: Hot Topic is not goth—it certainly emphasizes the darker edges of youth fashions and is alt music-oriented—but this doesn't make it goth.

Goodlad: I think very few self-identified goths, at least those old enough to drive a car, hang out or shop in malls. As with its punk subculture precursor, there's a certain presumption that if you're identified with goth you're going to put some effort into your goth-identified fashion. For some talented goths that might mean making their own clothing; for others it means finding things in thrift stores, antique clothing boutiques, the closets of older relatives, or specialty catalogues. All that said, I think that for some goths there may be a sense of amusement that stores like Hot Topic exist for the mass-marketing of a style that's supposed to be anti-mass: and obviously lots of people are buying those clothes or it wouldn't be a successful chain. For some it might be an indication of styles they'd better stop wearing!

MI: What is the significance of vampire fiction to goth subculture? How about the recent teen vampire fiction like the *Twilight* series?

Bibby: The recent interest in vampire lit is, of course, fueled by a Christian attempt to impose "just say no" cultural values on the genre. Its appeal is to white suburban youth, and it attempts to normalize the vampire genre—a genre that is not at all synonymous with goth. While many goths have a strong interest in vampire lit, most make a clear distinction between vampirism and goth.

Du Plessis: There is an interesting shift here, to whatever is and has been interesting about the idea of being a vampire. Maybe what's happening here is that there is such a larger contingent of gothic fiction that this type of fiction can now exist on many levels. *Twilight* is gothic for the really mainstream. [*Twilight*] is a break with Rice's vampire and the new millennial vision of vampires; immortality as a way of being a kid in high school forever.

MI: What roles do sex and sexuality play in goth culture?

Bibby: I recall that back in the mid-80s most goths I knew were determinedly asexual. Many I knew thought that sex was disgusting and ungoth. That's obviously changed—and it might have way more to do with the particular scene I knew—but I have seen the motif of the asexual goth crop up in numerous other manifestations of the subculture over the years. Because so much of contemporary goth draws its aesthetics from bondage subcultures, there seems to be much more emphasis on sex and sexualities. It also seems that contemporary goth bands tend to emphasize sexual display and style more than the first bands—some early goth bands self-consciously turned away from their audiences and refused to spectacularize their bodies by wearing dark, shapeless clothes, using a lot of fog and lighting that obscured them—Batcave bands, Siouxsie, and Bauhaus being more glam oriented, always played up sexuality—more recent bands tent to emphasize a sexually attractive lead singer and play out transgressive sex roles on stage.

Du Plessis: I thought, as participant-observer in goth from approximately the early 1980s to the late 1990s, that a very theatrical staging of non-normative sexualities (bisexual, "queer," fetishist, S & M) played a key role in goth. I think that with the general shift in the mainstreaming and packaging of lesbian and gay identities, along with the massive reinforcement of traditional sex/gender/sexuality norms in the last decade, sexuality is less now to goth. The near-disappearance of bisexuality (except in the most commoditized forms) and androgyny from almost all areas of popular culture are both cause and effect of the waning of the roles of sexuality and sex in goth.

MI: Where is goth going? What is in store for the future of the subculture?

Bibby: My guess is that the culture is aging—it's become so internet-oriented that it's almost become a kind of SCA (Society for Creative Anachronism) sort of subculture that attracts middle-aged techies more than young people.

Goodlad: Goth is as undead as it ever was. There will always be something that someone wants to claim for goth—or something that some group of people is claiming that those few who still call themselves goth will think they recognize as goth. It doesn't matter, in other words, whether it's goth, or dark culture, or emo, or what have you. At least for late-capitalist societies in which the young and the not so young have the leisure and the prosperity to explore the pleasures of self-aestheticization, there will be goth, it will stylize itself as dark and outré, and those who celebrate it will feel that they've found something so beautiful (or rare, or erratic, or meaningful) which they've managed to carve out from the everyday, that for them it will stand for what other people think of as spirituality.

(Interviews conducted by Micah Issitt and used by permission. Michael Bibby interview conducted November 17, 2009; Lauren M. E. Goodlad interview conducted May 9, 2010, and June 9, 2010; Michael Du Plessis interview conducted June 10, 2010.)

Joshua Gunn and Goth Music Research

In the following excerpt from the article "Goth Music and the Inevitability of Genre," Assistant Professor Joshua Gunn, with the University of Texas at Austin, discusses the categorization of popular music and the formation of "genres" in the course of musical discourse. Many of the bands both historically and currently categorized as "goth" bands have complicated relationships with the label. On one hand, their desire to be unique and individual makes them shrink from categorization of any kind, while on the other hand, the fact that they are known as a goth band means that their music will be identifiable to audiences who know they like goth music.

Gunn argues that, while it is possible to create "antigeneric" music, or music that falls outside of any single "genre," the music is quickly placed within a category both because of fans' need to talk about the music and because the music will ultimately need to be associated with other types of music for the purpose of sales, advertisement, and other necessities of music distribution and appreciation.

Gunn has a background in rhetorical research and theory and brings a unique view to his work on goth music. His articles have appeared in books like *Goth: Undead Subculture* and in a variety of other collections and scholarly journals.

Excerpts from the Conclusion Section of "Gothic Music and the Inevitability of Genre"

No one musical group serves as a perfect representative of any musical genre, and yet, just as some fans would suggest that the Sex Pistols are a punk band, so too would many claim that the Swans are a gothic band. Although it may be possible that an antigeneric music could exist, inevitably the discussions of fans, artists and disinterested auditors of musical creations negotiate meanings and generate adjectival codes that serve to fix the music in relation to existing and previously signified music. For instance, when the classically trained composer John Cage brought us Indeterminancy in 1959, people did not know what to make of the work. Yet by the time his second album appeared in the mid-Sixties, his work was easily tagged with the labels "classical minimalism" and "avant-garde," no doubt as a result of the metadiscursive moves of fans, artists, and critics. Likewise, Bauhaus's "strange" debut single soon elicited the "gothic" label, one which the band worked to evade throughout their career, yet never managed to escape.

Adjectival codes and the logics of canonizing are pivotal discursive processes in the discussions of fans and artists that both establish and expand the boundaries of gothic. These two elements of generic discourse, however, do not exhaust the producerly activity that contributes to generic negotiations and generic struggles. (Fashion, codes of behavior at gothic venues, and so on also play a role.) Nevertheless, they do suggest that the attempts of artists and fans to engage in discussions outside of generic discourse, to avoid categorizing, are ultimately futile. Because of the necessity of the adjective in describing and discussing music, and the inevitable associations between past and present musics, there is no "outside" space in which a particular musical work can evade metadiscursive negotiation. Because of the passing of time central to these two processes, there is no such thing as antigeneric music.

It could be argued, however, that when new and unanticipated musical forms are initially experienced, initially heard, there is at least an antigeneric moment. Even so, I believe such moments are ultimately incomprehensible ... Walser notes that "many artists bridle at genre categories because they see them as restrictive stereotypes, implying formulaic composition," yet often elide the fact that they are subject to "conflicting valorizations of audiences" and commercial strategies that inevitably lead to generic labels. The fact remains that, if we are to discuss our experience of a particular musical work, lest we utter a series of grunts we inevitably resort to our pragmatic, and inevitable, logic of categorization. In regard to music, this logic is often enacted with the aid of the adjective, which in turn serves as the ground for metadiscursive negotiations of meaning and value that privilege certain adjectival codes. We mark boundaries on the basis of similarity and difference, either immediately after our musical encounter (using the adjective), or in making reference to the past (identifying similar bands or artists).

(Excerpt from Gunn, Joshua. "Goth Music and the Inevitability of Genre." *Popular Music and Society*, 23 [1999]: 31–50. © 2009 Sage Publications. Used by permission of Joshua Gunn and Taylor & Francis Publishers.)

Goth Media

Goth media fills an importance niche within the culture, helping to disseminate information about emerging artists, fashion trends, and other cultural developments. In another sense, goth magazines and Web-based media help goths to feel that they are part of an extended community. An American goth magazine might, for instance, cover new bands coming from the Netherlands or might have an exposé on goth fashion in Japan. These articles help to foster a sense of belonging and perhaps for some goths importance in taking part in an international underground scene.

The goth music and culture magazine *New Grave* was published from 2000 to 2003, but produced only five issues. Publisher, writer, and creator Matt Riser, a longtime participant in the scene, decided there was not a magazine publishing the kinds of articles he wanted to see, and he decided to do it himself. Over the years, Riser took his time with each issue, ensuring that each issue contained something that other magazines did not carry. *New Grave* was the first magazine, for instance, to get an exclusive interview with one of the elusive Japanese visual kei bands, Dir en grey.

In addition to being a publisher and writer, Riser was also the founder of Fear Cult, a Los Angeles–based goth-rock band that gained a significant following in the national goth scene after more than 10 years of playing and recording, including the two full-length albums *A Bouquet of Songs* (1994) and *Your Darkest Romance* (1996) and the EP *Drop Dead* (1999).

The goth culture magazine *The Chronicles* began publication in 1996 out of London. The magazine was an extension of the London Vampyre Group.

Fashion for the Goth Reader

One way that goth magazines function within the subculture is by providing examples and instructions on how to achieve the goth look. Through photos and descriptions, readers encounter new ideas and get a glimpse of how the aesthetic manifests in different ways throughout the goth world. For goths in small communities, magazines and Internet sites may be their only access to the wider world of goth fashion. The magazines also provide commentary on goth fashion, examining both the development of the fashion scene and the significance of fashion in goth community.

Cassandra Ngo, 16, dressed as a "Gothic Lolita," draws an underground Operative System girl "2Ktan" character, July 3, 2004, at the Anime Expo 2004 (AX2004) at the Anaheim Convention Center in Anaheim, California. (AP Photo/Damian Dovarganes)

In the following articles from *New Grave* magazine, Matt Riser provides both instructions on how to achieve a "goth look" and a window into international goth fashion, through the style of Harajuku Street in Japan. The third article, from author Sue Jones, as printed in *The Chronicles*, takes a look at what the author sees as a growing disparity between goth culture and fashion, and the final article, from author Tara Daynes, writing in *The Chronicles*, examines the blend of fetish and goth styles and lifestyles.

"Harajuku"

During the busy work week, the area of Tokyo known as Harajuku is like any other normal, quiet, and sophisticated section of town, however when the weekend comes, the state is set for two of the most stunning and interesting phenomena in the history of fashion. I am referring to the Cosplayers and Gothic Lolitas. Teens and young adults come out of the countryside and from all areas of town to meet and socialize in their "Sacred Place." Instead of the typical announcement from the train conductor, a female voice sings "Harajuku, Harajuku" as the JR line arrives at its destination. From that peculiar announcement alone, you know that you have just arrived somewhere special.

On a Sunday afternoon, assuming the weather permits, the street is swarmed with Cosplayers (short for costume players) displaying their near-exact replica costumes, and sporting the hair and make-up of their favorite rockstars. These costumes are often made completely from scratch and painstakingly detailed so that every feature and nuance will be as close to the original as possible. The equivalent of hundreds of American dollars are spend on their outfits, and there has even become such a demand for them, that certain companies have begun producing replica costumes for cosplayers to purchase.

A slightly different style, but equally as expensive as Cosplay, is the style of Gothic Lolita, also known as the Elegant Gothic Lolita, or EGL for short. Despite the term "Gothic" being used in the title, this fashion trend has very little if anything to do with the "gothic rock" scenes in Europe and America. This Japanese fashion is more closely related to that of the Visual Kei movement and with visual rock bands, however, it is not exclusive to the visual scene. There are many EGL's that attend traditional non-visual gothic rock parties and concerts in Japan (keep in mind that visual rock is not looked upon highly among most Japanese goth rockers).

Currently alongside the Cosplayers, this "Lolita" fashion has become the most popular and demanding style among the Harajuku scenesters. It is so popular that there has even been three magazine style books published, entitled "Gothic & Lolita Bible," that follow and promote the trend.

Why Harajuku? Why not some other location? What makes this the "Sacred Place?" Once upon a time, Harajuku was known for its street performers and curbside curiosities. During the late 70's and early 80's, the streets were dominated by fashionable street gangs such as "Takenoko-zoku" and the "Rollers." Takenoko-zoku were kids who dressed only in clothes from the store Takenoko, and the Rollers were dressed only in 1950s rock-and-roller fashions, hence their name. These gangs would choreograph dances and perform them on their claimed territory of Harajuku. Always fighting among themselves over turf and boundary lines. In addition to these two gangs there were other fashionable gangs such as "Glam." With no interest in side dancing, "Glam" were a group of fashion and music minded youth who worked at prominent clubs like "Byblos" (located in Akasaka, and was where all the popular overseas musicians would hang out when touring Japan) and clothing stores such as "Gypsy Eye" (located in the Harajuku Plaza, a building which was torn down in the late 80's). It was out of such street gangs bands like Visual Scandal (often thought to be where the term "visual rock" comes from), Actress, Chanel, Etc., were born. Harajuku was an area that bands could set up and perform with hopes of being heard and getting noticed; a street of dreams for the would-be performers and wannabe rockstars. It was toward the end of these times, on a certain bridge, that a certain young band would set up and perform in full visual costume for the passers by. That band happed the legendary X-Japan (indisputably the most famous of all visual rock bands).

So, it is only natural that it is here, in Harajuku, that the youth come to pay their respect, display their fandom, and search for their own dreams to come true, and it only makes sense that they too, dress for the occasion. In this respect, Harajuku truly is a "sacred place."

(Riser, Matt. "Harajuku," *New Grave*, Issue 4, 2002: 18–19. © 2010 New Grave. Used by permission of Matt Riser.)

Excerpts from "In Case You Don't Have an Older Sister"

Some call it "teasing," some call it "back combing," whatever the case may be, it is the essential technique to achieving that "big hair" look. The important thing to know is that it is a technique anyone can learn. Too often I hear, "Oh, my hair doesn't tease well." Not true . . . everyone who has hair can tease it, if they know how. It just requires the right tools and a little practice.

1. The first step is to grab a hand full of hair and hold it straight up, or to a slight angle creating a downward slope for the brushing. Despite the name "back combing," an actual comb is not always the best tool for the job. I've discovered that a small Goody (a brand name for inexpensive hair products) brush is the best way to go.

2. While holding on tight to your hair, gently push the brush into the hair. Do not start too close to the top of the hair, it is best to begin about midway from your hand to your scalp. You will be brushing down toward the scalp.

3. As you brush down, brush as far down to the scalp as possible, and then pull the brush straight out at a right angle. Do this a few times with each patch of hair you hold up.

One you have teased a few patches of hair you will begin to notice that your hair is taking on a new life. It is suddenly able to be sculpted and shaped in ways that defy gravity. Once you have teased your hair and have shaped it into the desired look, you should begin to use some hair spray to make your creation stay. Avoid spraying too much hair spray toward the tips, it will cause the hair to get too heavy and it will want to fall down. Instead spray near the roots, this is where all the support will need to be.

When combing the hair out, you will need to start at the very tips of the hair and slowly work your way toward the scalp. Be patient and careful not to break or damage your hair. With a little patience, and by starting at the very ends of your hair, you will discover even the most tangled rat's nest will easily comb out. Also, make sure you use lots of conditioner when washing out the hair spray.

OK, that's it . . . you have just learned the tricks of the trade and are now ready to join the ranks of Robert Smith, Johnny Slut, and the members of Motley Crue. Enjoy your new look and if it didn't work the first time keep practicing and following these simple steps.

(Riser, Matt. "In Case You Don't Have an Older Sister," *New Grave*, Issue 4, 2002: 21. © 2010 New Grave. Used by permission of Matt Riser.)

"Do Clothes Maketh the Goth?"

I have been going to the Whitby Goth Weekend for quite a few years and I have noticed the growing phenomenon of people going to Whitby just to dress up, pose, and be photographed. They seem to know nothing of Goth culture, music or lifestyle.

We often encounter newcomers to Whitby who happen across the Goth Weekend and they ask a few questions like "what is it all about?" then they buy a couple of black t-shirts from the market and go home dressed as they came. Six months later they turn up in Whitby again with a car full of snazzy outfits, black jewellery and top hats all bought from the One Stop Goth Shop.

Often their outfits are more akin to the sort of outfits you can hire from fancy dress shops. You know the sort: cheap, thin satin, bad quality lace and hats adorned with brightly coloured feathers. You see them parading around Whitby in couples in matching outfits. They wear co-ordinating jewellery and carry matching walking sticks. This last WGW I was asked by someone if there were certain colours for certain days as they had seen several couples out and about in the same combination of colours! The motive of these people seems purely to be seen, to pose for photographs and to get their image in the Whitby Gazette. In the most recent Goth Weekend pullout from the Whitby Gazette several "Goths" featured admitted to "not being a Goth" and coming to Whitby "just to dress up" for a couple of days. Are these people Goths? Do they know what Goth is? Where were they when we sacked Rome?

I am talking about folk who are not active in the Goth community. They are not members of any group or club, never support any Goth event/meetings/social gatherings or subscribe to any Goth magazine that is aimed at our subculture. But because they stand out in the crowd so clearly they are usually used by Joe Public to measure what a real Goth should be. So, how do we define a Goth? Do Goths have to have dyed hair, multiple piercings and tattoos? Does wearing a pair of New Rocks make you a Goth? Does having a preference for wearing black or purple clothing, silver jewellery and lots of black eyeliner make you Goth?

I know individuals who display none of the above affectations but are Goth through and through, indeed if you broke these people in half they would have GOTH written all the way through like a Gothic stick of rock. Many people go through a Goth phase when young but true Goths never grow out of this phase indeed they submerge themselves in the culture and revel in it. Indeed lots of my Goth friends love to dress to impress but they dress for themselves and not just to draw attention to themselves.

I know people who do not consider themselves to be Goths instead they describe themselves as "alternative" and in doing so create another niche in this varied and eclectic subculture, which in turn adds to a varied and rich culture.

Goths dress in clothes to please themselves but pseudo Goths tend to wear clothes to please others and often try to out-Goth each other. I have experienced the "Gother than thou" attitude from pseudo Goths, which has been directed towards myself and others close to me. I accept that everyone has a right to go to Whitby, dress how they want and even indulge in a spot of posing but I feel true Goths go to Whitby to be themselves, pseudo-Goths go to Whitby to be someone else.

I consider myself a Goth, I even have a t-shirt with it printed on the front so it must be true. But I consider being a Goth as something, which comes from within. It is a personality trait that is with you from childhood, something you feel but cannot describe until you discover others who feel the same. And you learn the term Goth and come to realise it is a word that describes you and the way you see and interact with the world around you. It (darkly) colours many things in your life and you feel it is how you express your true self. What do you think, do clothes maketh the Goth?

(Jones, Sue, as originally printed in *The Chronicles*, Volume 2, No. 8, March 2008. Used by permission of Mick Smith. © 2010.)

"Kinky Sex, Please—We're Goths"

There has long been a cross-over between the gothic and fetish scenes. Much of it is the aesthetics and the joys of wearing fetish gear. It has to be said, we carry off PVC, latex, leather, corsets, stockings, stiletto heels, piercings etc far better than your average balding bank manager or portly middle-aged housewife, and we certainly aren't going to cover the immaculate eyeliner with some gimp mask.

But not only do we look the part, we want to show that we can walk the talk, and that our kinkiness is not just limited to our fashion statements. So, we buy Skin Two mag, we go to Torture Garden and the Rubber Ball, we wave our whips and riding crops about at parties and use them ostentatiously on mates (but not too hard). We boast loudly about how much we beat up our boyfriends or girlfriends (or both, if we really want to impress) in bed (or on a tombstone or dangling from the wardrobe or wherever). We dance suggestively with and/or snog our same-sex mates in the middle of the dancefloor. In short, we wear a virtual T-shirt bearing the logo 'Vanilla schmanilla!' on the front, because after all, there is no kudos to be had in the missionary position.

But how much of all this is genuine kinkiness, and how much of it is just for effect? Are we really that into BDSM, bisexuality etc and all that goes with it? Or if we went to a 'real' fetish club with hardcore players, how many of us would poop our PVC pants at what really goes on? Do we really like pain so much, or do we just like to proudly show off the scars, the scratchmarks, the ropeburns, like a badge of honour? And do we honestly want to be tied to the bed and choked during sex, or do we secretly yearn for tenderness, affection, cuddles and a nice back rub?

For many of us Goths, being non-scene, and consequently non-seen, is not an option. Not only do we want to belong and be accepted, we want to be admired and revered by our gothic peers. But when so many of us already look so fantastic in our tight and shiny fet gear, in order to really make an impact, we feel obliged to go that step further and be noticed by our actions as well as for our outfits.

But being kinky isn't a compulsory requirement for being a goth, any more than is having a sad and desperate need to shock. I know that there are genuine PervyGoths out there (most of whom actually keep their personal and private hobbies in this regard far more personal and private). And I think people pretending to share their predilections just for show is as much of an insult to them as someone putting on a Black Rose dress and claiming that makes them a Goth, is to the rest of us.

Part of having a sub-cultural identity is about being true to yourself in spite of other people's views. So surely we should be comfortable with who we are and what we do or don't do, and not feel we have to push the envelope to such a drastic extent in order to gain the approval and esteem of our peers—we leave that to the mainstream crowd!

And anyway, the rest of us know the score and are just rolling our eyes and smirking about it behind our hands anyway.

(Daynes, Tara. "Kinky Sex Please—We're Goths," as originally printed in *The Chronicles*, Volume 2, No. 8, March 2007. Used by permission of Mick Smith. © 2010.)

The Subcultural Marketplace

Vendors marketing to goth audiences often concentrate their advertising on goth magazines, Web sites, and concerts. In the 1980s and early 1990s, vendors relied on mail-order business to sell to goths living in far-flung locations. With the advent of Internet sales, specialty vendors are now able to reach a national and even international audience through online stores.

While specialty vendors use goth magazines to reach their target audiences, the editors and writers of the magazines are also on the lookout for products that appeal to goths, whether sold by small independent producers or by national or international companies.

In the short article "Gothic Barbie," *New Grave* magazine finds a mainstream product that might appeal to goth audiences. As a subculture with a devoted interest in fantasy, goths are an excellent audience for the dark alternative playthings that serve as conversation pieces in a gothic home. The next article is a review of a graphic novel from Blackest Heart Media, a literary adaptation of the classic 1970s zombie film from filmmaker Lucio Fulci. This article provides an example of how horror literature and alternative literature like graphic novels find an audience within the goth community.

Artist and designer Norie Ayukawa provides an example of the magazine-style advertisements for her unique jewelry and accessories marketed under the name Hyde's Vice. In the short interview provided, Norie discusses her ideas about marketing to goth audiences and what makes goth audiences a unique market.

"Gothic Barbie"

As an attempt to make a more perfect Barbie, I believe it is fair to say that most of us have, at some point in our gothic existence, created our own death-rock Barbie. Altering her boring blond façade into a stunning gothic dream come true. Coloring her hair, enhancing her makeup and constructing her wardrobe to better match our own. Well, Mattel has just made our work a little bit easier, for they have released "gothic" Barbie.

OK, so it's not exactly "gothic" Barbie, it's actually much cooler than that. It's Barbie and Ken made to celebrate the genius of Charles Addams. This pair of dolls resemble the Addams family characters of

Morticia and Gomez. Modeling their hair, makeup and outfits after those found in the original comic strip, TV series and feature length films. We see Ken in Gomez's trademark pinstriped suite and sleazy mustache, while Barbie showcases the low cut, tight fitting funeral gown, complete with the long flowing tattered sleeves, and ground slithering tentacle-like bottom.

This creepy couple was released just in time for Halloween with a suggested retail price of $79.00. These dolls are suggested for ages 14 and up, but I would go ahead and buy it for your child anyway . . . so what if they choke on the small parts . . . it's nothing compared to the toys that Pugsley and Wednesday play with.

(Riser, Matt. "Gothic Barbie," *New Grave*, Issue 2, 2000: 23. Used by permission of Matt Riser and *New Grave*. © 2010 New Grave.)

"Lucio Fulci's Zombie"

Still warm off the presses comes ZOMBIE; the latest offering from Blackest Heart Media. A graphic (by all meanings of the word) novel celebrating Lucio Fulci's popular cult/horror/gore film of the late 70's. This release is written by Stephen Romano, and illustrated by Michael Broom, with inking done by the talents of Derek Rook and Gerry Coffey. Also included with this release is a digitally remastered CD soundtrack of the film.

I'll admit it has been a while since I let my self get drawn in to a comic book, and I had no real intentions to review such things in this magazine. However, when copies of THE BEYOND and ZOMBIE arrived in my box, I was somewhat intrigued. It's hard to ignore something of quality. From start to finish it is apparent that this is not some cheap attempt to make a buck off some sorry Fulci fan who needs to own all things Fulci. Instead we have what is an inspired product that is obviously made by fans for fans. No noticeable sacrifice in expense or production has been made. Instead, we have a well adapted story that is showcased by amazing illustrations. The kind of illustrations that are energized with character and personality. Very similar to the macabre illustration style of Berni Wrightson. Where faces look like faces, and not some stylized "learn to draw comics in the Marvel way" faces. Characters actually have character. The artwork comes alive (or shall I say undead) to carry the reader through the mature dialogue presented by Romano.

From what I understand, Romano has been trying to remake this classic Fulci film for some time. Finding it more than difficult to fund such an elaborate project. He has instead received a temporary fix by taking his ideas to the comic medium. Not to say the dream of a modern film remake has been abandoned, but rather set aside for the time being. He tackled the project with as much passion and enthusiasm as he would if he were making a film. Carefully hand selecting the artists as one would cast actors or hire directors. It is this attention to detail and the passion that must go behind such an endeavor that is ever so apparent with this release.

To accompany your reading, there is a 30 track CD soundtrack which includes the film's original score as well as other rarities. This wonderful inclusion contains 12 remastered tracks of music composed and performed by Fabio Frizzi and Giorgio Tucci. There are alternate versions of songs as well as two tracks of remixed songs. In addition to the film's soundtrack, Blackest Heart has provided a supplement containing songs by rokOpera and Cinema Strange Orchestra. Also contained for your listening pleasure is original radio advertisements that were used to promote the Fulci film. Both the film score and the Radio spots have been remastered. Exposing only slightly indictable aging and deterioration of the original soundtrack. I like the whole idea of including a soundtrack with a graphic novel. It really adds a whole other layer and mood to the reading experience. I hope to see more of such things in the future.

(Riser, Matt. "Lucio Fulci's Zombie." *New Grave*, Issue 1, 2000: 12. Used by permission of Matt Riser and New Grave. © 2010, New Grave.)

Hyde's Vice

MI: How did you design the advertisement for Hyde's Vice?
Ayukawa: Probably the most usual colors used in ads intended for a gothic audience are red, purple and black, and ours was no exception. The font of the logo was intended to look elegant and vintage, keep the Victorian feel of the cameo. But we thought that the rest of the writing should be bold and easy to read, do what an ad is supposed to do. We also utilized the ransom note style graphics to the bold font in order to give the ad a little punk rock edge.

Advertisement for Hyde's Vice. (Used by permission of Norie Ayukawa and Hyde's Vice. © 2010 Hyde's Vice.)

MI: What kind of publications/other venues do you use to advertise your products?

Ayukawa: So far we have advertised through *Deathrock* magazine, Dances of Vice festival, and the local Punk Rock flea market. Dances of Vice exposed the brand to the Steam Punk audience and the Punk Rock flea market to locals.

MI: Are there other markets of consumers outside of goth culture appropriate for your products?

Ayukawa: Hyde's Vice accessories are worn by anybody with a little bit of an edge. Most young people are wearing skulls now so I do get customers from every walk of life.

MI: What are your thoughts about marketing to goths? What types of products to goths like?

Ayukawa: We are not trying to make products that appeal to a specific market, but I think that the product just lends itself to be marketed to goths, punk rockers, and other alternative people of all sorts since it has that little macabre aspect. The market is so wide and can get into a lot of specifics—not everything can be "one size fits all"—but skulls are a definite plus.

(Used by permission of Norie Ayukawa and Hyde's Vice. © 2010 Hyde's Vice.)

Goth Music and the Media

One of the primary functions of the goth media is to spread the word about goth music throughout the community. An emerging artist whose music might be well accepted within goth circles (whether or not they personally accept the label) needs to find an audience, and this requires marketing their music through specialty publications, Web sites, and through word of mouth by distributing at goth venues. Most goth magazines focus first on music reviews and interviews and only then on fashion and other aspects of the culture. An exception to this is the magazine *Gothic Beauty*, which began publication in 2000 and focuses on fashion first, though they also advertise and promote goth music.

The goth music industry also requires both record labels willing to sign new artists and distributors who want to focus on promoting goth artists. In the twenty-first century, success in music distribution requires the ability to both market and sell music in electronic format, and most labels and distribution companies today make Internet marketing a cornerstone of their business.

Projekt Records

Sam Rosenthal, founder of Projekt Records and the goth-eseque band Black Tape for a Blue Girl, has been producing and promoting music in the broader goth genres since the 1980s. Starting with the promotion of his own music, he moved on to sign a number of artists now popular within the extended community. Rosenthal's distribution business began as a mail-order company, then transitioned into Web marketing, and now uses both methods to reach the largest possible audience.

Like most distribution companies and labels, Projekt markets more than simply goth bands in the traditional vein, and has branched out to include a number of unique and interesting musical acts that blur the lines between genres. Rosenthal has continued creating and marketing his own music, while building Projekt into one of the most well-known and trusted sources for new bands in the industry. Mix CDs produced by Projekt: Darkwave provide listeners with exposure to a variety of new acts emerging from communities across the United States and extended into the European scene.

In the following interview, Rosenthal explains how he became involved with Projekt, how the label gained its reputation, and about the current state of goth culture and music.

Interview with Sam Rosenthal

MI: Can you describe your introduction to goth culture and decision to become involved in producing music?
Rosenthal: I got involved in music before I had any knowledge of what the goth scene was. I released my first cassette of solo electronic/ambient music in 1983. Over the next few years, I discovered music on the 4AD label. Bands like The Cocteau Twins, Dead Can Dance, This Mortal Coil.

Here in the U.S., it wasn't called "Goth." It was just weird, dark, moody music coming out of England. In 1986, I released "The Rope," the first album from my band Black Tape for a Blue Girl. To me, it was dark electronic music, influenced as much by Brian Eno as Soft Cell or This Mortal Coil.

As I sent out promo copies of the Vinyl LP, I noticed positive responses coming from one group, and deafening silence from others.

The people who were responding enthusiastically were what we'd now call "Goths." They were the magazines and fanzines and Djs who were also writing about The Cure, Siouxsie, Love & Rockets, Christian Death. So that is really when I discovered the Goth scene. In 1986, I lived in Orange County, CA, at college. There were shows happening up in Los Angeles, but I was unaware of that at the time; I still felt isolated, making my own sound. The next Blacktape album, "Mesmerized by the Sirens," came out in 1987. It was even more This Mortal Coil-y than the first. More acoustic guitar, strings, female vocals. It never was what you'd traditionally call "goth," because I think Bauhaus or Siouxsie or the Sisters capture the traditional sound, with a rock band lineup.

Projekt: Darkwave began in the early 90s. The Projekt label was already happening, with numerous releases, and I was selling a lot of music by mail-order. I began importing records from Europe, to sell to my fans, and also to stores. I started carrying local goth labels like Tess Records. That was how Projekt: Darkwave came together.

MI: What were some of the first bands associated with your label?

Rosenthal: Of course, Black Tape for a Blue Girl was the first. In 1989, I released a "best of" from Attrition. There was Peyote from O Yuki Conjugate, another UK act. Then I started signing new American bands I discovered like Lycia, Love Spirals Downwards, Lovesliescrushing, Soulwhirlingsomewhere. Those four, along with Blacktape, are really the original Projekt acts.

MI: Who are some of the most prominent bands associated with your label?

Rosenthal: Well, it kind of depends on what era of Projekt you are talking about. From the Los Angeles days (through 1995), it was Blacktape, Lycia, and Love Spirals Downwards. From the Chicago days (1996–1999), it was Blacktape, Voltaire, Lycia. From the Queens, NY, days (2000–2002) it was Blacktape, Mira, and Voltaire. The early Brooklyn era (2003–2006) was Android Lust, Voltaire. And now, in the Gowanus Brooklyn era (2007-present), we're having success with Blacktape, Lovesliescrushing, and some of the newer signees like Tearwave and The Twilight Garden.

MI: How do you feel Projekt: Darkwave contributes or fits into the contemporary scene?

Rosenthal: Well, Projekt (the label) has been putting out releases for 28 years. Projekt: Darkwave has been a mail-order company for about

18 years. What we have is longevity. We've been in touch with many generations of fans of the genre, and we keep up with what they are looking for.

Many good labels have come and gone in that period, and some that are still around have changed their focus. Projekt keeps making good music available. As far as my own role: I am sort of a filter, in that when I hear a band that I think rises above the crowd, I sign them to Projekt. This is something that the label's fans understand, "Ok, Sam is recommending this band, because he's putting his money and time into them." I serve as a signpost for what I think is worth hearing. Naturally, not everyone will agree with my tastes. . . . but there are many people who do, so that works out for all of us: band, label, and fan.

MI: From your perspective, what are some of the major milestones in the development of the U.S. goth scene?

Rosenthal: Unfortunately the main one that sticks in mind is not a positive thing, but rather when the U.S. Goth scene started to shrink. That was the period between Rozz Williams' suicide (April 1998) and Columbine (April 1999). I don't really think those two things had anything to do with the decline, but that was the time frame for the end of a golden era.

I think that time also ties into the decline of retail stores, the point where the Internet/napster/digital really took hold. It used to be that any obscure CD Projekt released had a good chance of selling 1000-2000 copies in stores. A decade later, the same CD can only sell 300-500 in stores.

MI: How has goth music changed since the beginning?

Rosenthal: It has definitely diversified. So many other things are part of the goth sound, whether it be synth pop, or EBM, or metal, or ethereal. In 1982, none of that was really part of it. Goth was just a little bit more than a glam rock band with a dark sound.

MI: What are some of the most important or interesting subgenres popular today?

Rosenthal: My favorite current subgenre is Dark Cabaret. These bands bring in a 1920's Weimar-Republic element. You can see it in Dresden Dolls, Revue Noir, Jill Tracy, the Deadfly Ensemble, Adrian H and the Wounds, etc.

MI: What are the primary elements that make a band fit into the "goth" label?

Rosenthal: I don't really think you can describe one primary element. Goth is whatever goth fans say it is. I suspect it comes more from the mood of the music than the instrumentation or arrangements. It's music that is dark, introspective, a bit moody and unsettling. But there are so many different bands that people call goth. You cannot really nail it down.

MI: What are some of the major features of the goth lifestyle or general attitude?

Rosenthal: The goths that I know exist in the mainstream world, by being pilots, IT people, designers, V.P.s of marketing. I don't think Goth is a culture that people can exist in exclusively. Very few people make a living just by being a promoter, booking agent, artist, or label owner. In that sense, I am very lucky. My full-time job is running Projekt. That gives me the freedom to work less than most people, and spend more time with my son, or in the studio creating my art. I do not feel that Goth culture can be "in opposition" to mainstream culture, because it is a way that people choose to express themselves within society. It is not like goths go off and start a "goth commune" where they only behave "gothly" all the time (laughs)!

(Interview conducted by the author on March 9, 2010. Used by permission of Sam Rosenthal.)

Music Reviews

Albums produced by labels like Projekt are eventually shopped around the goth magazines and Web sites for review. A good review in a trusted magazine can dramatically boost sales, especially for a fledgling band that's only starting to generate any kind of excitement.

The following short reviews provide an example of how goth magazines describe music for their audiences. Obtaining reviews of this kind can be a major milestone for an emerging goth band, while established bands also depend on reviews to promote their new releases and to reinforce the relevance to new generations of fans.

Review of Hellbent: Hardcore Vanilla

If you are curious as to what the future will sound like, I suggest you take a listen to this. Hellbent spews forth some 12 songs of pure technological genius. I wouldn't dare call it "industrial" for fear it would be an insult. I think every recorded track on this album was shoved through some sort of distortion filter; Harsh, gritty, raw, but beautiful. Like a computer raped pop song; bloody and violent, stripped down and naked. The compositions seem so natural and effortless, yet as you dig deep into their seemingly minimal structures, you find the most complex and detailed assembly.

Full of modern beats and stylings, everything from trip-hop to noise-funk. Whispery vocals, sometimes melodic, sometimes throaty with a certain sleaze factor, and in one case they are in French, and that's about it. I have a feeling this album was one big happy accident. The band should now break up, dress flashy, kill themselves, and go down in history as being revolutionary. Buy it, listen to it, and if you don't like it you're a damn fool.

(Riser, Matt. "Hellbent-Hardcore Vanilla." *New Grave*, Issue 3, 2001: 50. Used by permission of Matt Riser and New Grave. © 2010 New Grave.)

Review of Sanguis et Cinis—Alright. Let's Rock

The long awaited new release from these European dark/death/ glam-rockers. With their last album, there was a strong Sisters of Mercy "Vision Thing" type of sound. That style didn't really carry through to this release. This time around Sanguis takes on a sound that is perhaps more unique and individual to themselves. This time what we get is a creepy glam rock feel. A slower and more droning quality, with a dark guitar heaviness, and the occasional spooky keyboard melody to add more atmosphere. A raw sleazy rock n' roll quality seeps in and out of the production and presentation. Even the album title, and recent advertising campaigns have all alluded to this new direction. However, old fans of Sanguis need not worry, this new sound should be just as appealing and enjoyable as their last. After all, this band has always evolved and played with various styles, while remaining uniquely "Sanguis." And most likely that is the reason they are able to stay a step ahead of their competition.

(Riser, Matt. "Sanguis et Cinis—Alright. Let's Rock." *New Grave*, Issue 1, 2003: 64. Used by permission of Matt Riser and New Grave. © 2010 New Grave.)

Review of Songs of Terror: A Gothic Tribute to E. A. Poe

I know what you are thinking, "Not another tribute album!" Well my friends, this is not your typical tribute album. This one is to Edgar Allan Poe and these are not simply Poe's poems put to music; (at least they are not supposed to be, however some idiots can't follow directions and did it anyway.)

The songs, for the most part, are all original in lyrical and musical composition using a particular Poe poem or short story in mind for the inspiration. It's an interesting exercise with substantial results. On this compilation, we have 14 tracks featuring bands from all ranks of the gothic genre. For instance, there are a couple of old school acts like Kommunity FK and Ex-Voto with many modern day bands like Faith and the Muse, Cinema Strange and Fear Cult. All in all it's a total mix of style and backgrounds, with one common denominator, they are all fans of Poe. Even the artwork, done by yours truly, was a testament to his genius. So, if you're looking for a gothic compilation with an original twist or another item to put on your Poe shrine, there here it is.

(Riser, Matt. "Various Artists—Songs of Terror: A Gothic Tribute to E. A. Poe." *New Grave*, Issue 4, 2002: 54. Used by permission of Matt Riser and New Grave. © 2010 New Grave.)

Goth Literature

From the classics of gothic horror to modern vampire mysteries and gothic graphic novels, literature plays an important role in the evolving subculture. In addition to professional writers, playwrights, and poets, the subculture harbors a small army of amateur writers whose works are primarily published on cyberspace and on the pages of goth magazines. Short stories, essays, and poetry feature prominently among the works created by amateur goth literaries.

While an impressive range of amateur literature is produced by goths, there is considerable thematic and stylistic overlap. Many goth writers address supernatural themes and characters like vampires, werewolves, and undead creatures. Many also use their literature as a forum for introspection and to voice their thoughts about the subculture, the "outside" world, and life within it. In this way, goth fiction can provide an interesting window into the overall attitudes that bind people from across the world into the subculture.

Goth Poetry

The morbid and often awkwardly "moody" poetry produced by goths and would-be goths has become something of a joke within the goth community, as well as a stereotype familiar to many outside the subculture. Even so, given that a good poem can have as much, if not more, impact as a novel, some goths defy the clichés and take a stab at the genre.

The following poem was written by Ed St. Boniface and published in the pages of *The Chronicles Literary Supplement*. Boniface uses the character of a Raven, the familiar foil of poet Edgar Allan Poe, combined with gothic imagery in what appears a tribute to the classic themes of gothic fiction.

"The Raven's Lair"

> *I know a Raven*
> *With a grave and obscure purpose,*
> *His serious expression*
> *And weird profession*
> *Makes London verdurous*
> *With black ivies and bracken.*
>
> *I see him in vignette*
> *Narrated by Bosch;*
> *Engaged in projects*
> *Burdened with objects*
> *Unclear in the wash*
> *Of a polychrome Market.*
>
> *An ebony chess piece*
> *In a lurid tableau*
> *Occasionally stunning*
> *Certainly cunning*
> *Framed in the glow*
> *Of a surreal masterpiece.*

Flibbertigibbets and skeleton librettes
Are his signature;
Gargoyles grim
Converse with him
In apartments of pure
Grotesquerie and chilling secrets.

In this maddening gallery
Are frightening portraitures.
Grating babelesque tintamars
Rhythms of more haunted stars:
Much imagery that stirs
Apprehensive flattery.

Here waits the Raven in his lair
Serenading darkness
With unseen finesse
Courting metamorphosis
This strange being hearkens
Revelation's deadly glare.

(St. Boniface, Ed. "The Raven's Lair." As originally published in *The Chronicles Literary Supplement*, Volume 1, November 2003. Used by permission of Mick Smith. © 2010 The Chronicles.)

Vampire Stories

Supernatural themes have always been very popular in gothic literature, both for classic authors and also among modern gothic writers who have continued this tradition. While some "serious" goths reject vampire fiction, finding it a bit too theatrical, stories about vampires have long had a significant following within the subculture.

Over the years, vampire fiction has evolved into a genre of its own, from classic tales of undead vampires to modern approaches pinning vampires as everything from mutated humans infected by viral agents to a separate species evolved alongside *Homo sapiens* as predators.

The following excerpt from the story "Anything for a Friend," by writer J. Jones, was published in the British goth magazine *The Chronicles*. Jones's short story is an example of yet another take on vampire fiction, the dark-comedy approach, which has also been used to great effect by a number of modern novelists. In this story, Charlie and Jake, two British chums, make a bet with three of their friends that they can get through a night in a crypt, rumored to be the resting place of a vampire. Charlie finds himself needing to relieve his bladder and, as the rain is pouring outside, decides to do so in the rear of the crypt. That is when, to both men's amazement, a dark-clad figure emerges from the shadows.

Excerpt from "Anything for a Friend"

. . . And then suddenly everything happened at once. In an explosive frenzy a dark figure leapt up and in one movement grabbed Charlie by the throat, and I caught a flashing glance of what looked like a very long sharp pair of teeth. I jumped about a foot in the air.

Although I don't really believe in vampires (I was only here for the money), I had seen enough late night films on television to know what to do. I grabbed for my stump but it got tangled in my pants . . . . my trousers just weren't made for something this long and hard. I pulled at it frantically, trying to whip it out.

"Jake! Jake!" Charlie was screaming, frantically trying to get himself free. "Stop buggering about with yourself and get the bastard!" And then the stump came free, and I raised it for the kill. "Hey!" I yelled, "You with the teeth!" The vampire sort of paused in mid-strangle and turned towards me. That was all the opportunity I needed, and I launched myself like some graceful gazelle on the African Plains. It was like slow motion, quite poetic really. I landed beside the vampire and thrust my stump at his chest with all my body weight behind it.

Now then, if I might digress for a moment; in films, the stake always sort of glides through the vampire like a knife through hot butter (or is it the other way round?). Well anyway, I can categorically say to you without fear of any contradiction . . . no way! Either my knife wasn't hot enough or he definitely wasn't made of butter, because the stump made a loud thump as it hit him, and stopped dead as though I had tried to pierce a brick wall, with a shock wave that almost broke my wrists.

So there I was, still standing there clutching my weapon in both hands. The vampire however had un-strangled Charlie and had dropped to his knees like a stone, wheezing and gasping like an out of tune accordion.

Don't ask me why, but I dropped my stump, grabbed a handful of the vampire's hair and cut a chunk off with the scissors. Then I just made a bolt for the door (and no jokes about carpentry!). It was touch and go who would make it outside first, but Charlie beat me to it by half a yard. It's amazing just how much motivation fear can wring out of you. The rain was still absolutely torrential and we were completely soaked before we had gone more than a few yards from the crypt.

As we ran down towards the cemetery gates I held up the hair for Charlie to see. "Fifty quid!" I laughed, "You can have that pee now!"

"No thanks," Charlie said sheepishly, "Just had one, when the vampire grabbed me!"

"So what?" I laughed, "By the time we get to the gates we'll both be drenched to the skin, so what difference does it make?"

As we reached the gates we just dived into the back of Dave's car, next to Pete. "We did it!" Charlie grinned triumphantly, "Jake's got the hair, just hand over the dosh!!"

Pete and Dave just looked at each other. "Where's Clive?" Pete asked, and he seemed a bit concerned.

"What do you mean ... where's Clive?" Charlie snapped angrily. "Just hand over the fifty squids and let's bugger off, this place is way too weird for me!"

"No, no, no, you don't understand!" Pete was trying to calm Charlie down, "Clive was waiting for you in the crypt with all the gear on, make-up and everything. He was going to jump out on you and scare the crap out of you. It was a joke, to take the piss out of you both. Talking of which ... can anybody smell cat pee?"

"Oh shit!" I said despairingly, "We thought he was the mad vampire, I tried to shove a stake through his heart."

We all stared at each other for a long moment, then we all piled out of the car and ran over to the crypt. Clive lay face up on the grass outside the crypt, the rain beating down on him relentlessly. About six inches of cricket stump was sticking out of his chest.

"Oh Jesus!" Dave cried out, "He's dead! What have you done? You've bloody well killed him!" He and Pete were staring at me accusingly.

"No! no!" I yelled, panting with blind panic, "I didn't kill him, he was still alive when we left him. I didn't do that! No way! Tell them Charlie!"

But Charlie was kneeling beside Clive, inspecting something. He leaned back and pointed at what he had been looking at. On Clive's neck were two small puncture marks, still oozing two small dribbles of blood.

"NO!" I screamed wildly, unable to believe my eyes. "The vampire killed him, he killed Clive. And I'll tell you what, I'm going to have the bastard for doing this!"

I looked around wildly for something, anything I could use as a weapon. Only about fifteen feet away was a wheelbarrow and in it was a large gravediggers shovel. I ran over and snatched it from the wheelbarrow. "I'll show the bastard!" I screamed out. I was intent on getting revenge, to prove it was the vampire that killed Clive and not me.

Pete, Dave and Charlie were all walking towards me and then . . . . . . Clive got up and started to walk up behind them! They were all so intent on gibbering on about some joke or other they didn't see Clive coming up behind them. Except it wasn't Clive. No, Clive was dead, it was the vampire that was sneaking up behind them in Clive's body! I wasn't going to let any vampire get his hands on any more of my mates, so I just pushed through them and went for what used to be Clive.

The bugger was also going on about some joke or other, but I wasn't having any, oh no. It had killed my mate and now it was my turn. Oh yes, the murdering bastard had every right to look scared, I can tell you. I lifted the shovel and swung it with all my might.

This time it was just like in the movies. Clive's head was severed sweetly from his body and it curved high in the air, tumbling and spiraling, just like in slow motion, before falling to the ground beside his prostrate body . . . . YESSS!!

"That'll show the bugger!" I laughed, turning towards my mates. I expected relief, thanks even, but they just stood there looking at me with their mouths open.

Ungrateful sods!

(Jones, J. "Anything for a Friend." As originally printed in *The Chronicles Literary Supplement*, No. 2, December 2005. Used by permission of Mick Smith. © 2010 The Chronicles.)

Annotated Bibliography

Books

Baddeley, Gavin. *Goth Chic: A Connoisseur's Guide to Dark Culture*. Medford, NJ: Plexus, 2002.

    Baddeley's exploration of goth culture generally focuses on the culture's manifestation within pop culture media. Baddeley covers many of the biggest names in music, film, and literature and provides interesting and very readable commentaries on how each thing fits into the culture as a whole. The book's primary effect is to create an idea of the diversity of goth culture outside the picture typically provided by the mainstream media.

Brill, Dunja. *Goth Culture: Gender, Sexuality and Style*. New York: Berg, 2008.

    Brill begins her book with an excellent potted history of goth culture and a short look at how the culture appears around the world. From this point, she dissects the culture issue by issue, delving into elements of sexuality and style preference and exploring these aspects in relation to sociological theories of the present and the past. Brill's scholarship is admirable and her writing fluid, but this book is primarily of interest to those undertaking scholarly studies.

Godoy, Tiffany, and Ivan Vartanian. *Japanese Goth*. New York: Universe, 2009.

    Goth is a worldwide phenomenon, and this book provides a look at some of the ways that goth is represented in Japan. The Japanese goth scene is known for its extreme fashion, which includes several of the big subgroups, like "Gothic Lolita" and "cybergoth" and a range of blends in between. Godoy and Vartanian have produced an excellent set of photographs that are both beautiful and thought provoking and stand as an excellent document of goth's fashion evolution.

Goodlad, Lauren M. E., and Michael Bibby, eds. *Goth: Undead Subculture*. Durham, NC: Duke University Press, 2007.

This excellent collection of essays from editors Lauren Goodlad and Michael Bibby provides a thorough exploration of many facets of goth subculture. Most are written with the scholarly audience in mind, but the book provides interesting reading for the lay reader as well. The book covers music and the development of local goth scenes, and delves into the question of gender and identity with admirable detail. While the book does not provide exhaustive detail on any single issue in particular, many of the authors within feature prominently in the modern literature on goth and subcultures in general. This book is strongly recommended for students and general readers looking to understand more about the gothic subculture as it appears around the world.

Hebdige, Dick. *Subculture: The Meaning of Style*. New York: Routledge, 1981.

For anyone interested in a serious study of subculture, Hebdige's seminal work on the subject is a good place to start. While some of Hebdige's arguments may be seen as dated in the context of more recent work, it remains one of the best introductions to the subject. In addition, Hebdige does an excellent job of laying out the reasons that subcultures and the study of subcultures are important to sociology. Recommended for students of sociology, counterculture, and deviant behavior.

Hodkinson, Paul. *Goth: Identity, Style and Subculture*. New York: Berg, 2002.

Hodkinson is a goth turned researcher of goths, whose work has taken center stage as part of the primary literature on goth as a subculture. This book is the result of an extended study including interviews and observations of goths attending the Whitby Gothic Weekend. Hodkinson is a skilled researcher, and he takes great care in elucidating many different arguments on the nature of subculture before introducing his own well-thought-out theories on the significance of goth. Definitely recommended for anyone intending to study the sociology of subcultures.

Kilpatrick, Nancy. *The Goth Bible: A Compendium for the Darkly Inclined*. New York: St. Martin's Griffin, 2004.

Kilpatrick's book is written for the general reader and provides a wealth of information in an enjoyable and humorous package. The author divides her book into chapters focusing on fashion, drugs, music, sex, and the social aspects of the culture, always presenting information in an easily accessible and interesting way. Using interviews, historical summaries, and essays, the book touches on all the most important topics in gothdom and may be seen as one of the best introductions to what's out there. Kilpatrick is not a critical explorer, and though she pokes fun at the goths on many occasions, her book is a celebration of goth culture and the author never hides her admiration and unquestionable passion for all things goth.

Mercer, Mick. *The Hex Files: The Goth Bible*. New York: Overlook Press, 1996.
Mercer is one of the major figures in goth media. Through his books, his articles in various goth magazines, and his involvement in the net.goth newsgroups, Mercer has been a constant defender of goth culture, trying to counter some of the pervasive misconceptions that were distributed through the mainstream media. Mercer's *Hex Files* is a unique book, serving as a list of things that are goth. Grouped by country, Mercer compiled a list of people, organizations, bands, and books in the goth culture. While some of the bands and organizations listed may now be defunct, Mercer's snapshot of goth culture in 1996 is well worth a look.

Mercer, Mick. *21st Century Goth*. Richmond, UK: Reynolds and Hearn, 2002.
Mercer's updated goth bible for 2002 expands beyond the United States and the United Kingdom to provide information on goth stuff in a wider area. Mercer pays more attention to the Web in this third installment of his who's who series and therefore provides a useful resource to those doing research on goth culture, vampire, fetish, and other subgroups.

Reynolds, Simon. *Rip It Up and Start Again: Postpunk 1978–1984*. New York: Penguin, 2006.
A British music journalist by trade and music history buff from birth, Reynolds provides an interesting look at the landscape in the transformative musical period between punk and everything that came after. Though many of the bands mentioned will not fit under the goth banner, Reynolds's investigations elucidate how the musical stage was set for the emergence of goth as a genre distinct from the new wave and positive punk sounds.

Spooner, Catherine. *Contemporary Gothic*. New York: Reaktion Books, 2007.
Spooner conducts an in-depth analysis of the gothic aesthetic, focusing on those elements that, in her opinion, have helped maintain the counter-culture despite changes in the surrounding culture. An interesting study, written in accessible language and tone that seeks to neither criticize nor condemn but merely to understand and examine the appeal of goth around the world. Spooner is a skilled academic, but also reveals herself to be capable of writing analyses that are appropriate for the general reader.

Steele, Valerie, and Jennifer Park. *Gothic: Dark Glamour*. New Haven, CT: Yale University Press, 2008.
Steele and Park focus on fashion in this book, which covers the origins and development of goth fashion and its influence on mainstream style. Rich with photography, the book provides a visual exploration of dark fashion, with insightful commentary to supplement the photos.

Thompson, Dave. *The Dark Reign of Gothic Rock: In the Reptile House with The Sisters of Mercy, Bauhaus and The Cure*. London: Helter Skelter, 2002.
One of the few music books to deal specifically with goth music, Thompson's book is well written and fills an important niche in music history. Thompson begins with a look at the post-punk landscape, paying particular attention to

how bands like Joy Division and Siouxsie and the Banshees set the stage for what would become goth.

Venters, Jillian. *Gothic Charm School: An Essential Guide for Goths and Those Who Love Them.* New York: Harper, 2009.

Venters's charming book is something of a goth "how to" guide, covering subjects ranging from fashion to hitting the nightlife for entertainment. The book is organized as a sort of etiquette guide for goths, answering many questions goths may have developed about how to navigate their daily lives while remaining goth. An entertaining and informative read by a very imaginative and skilled author.

Voltaire. *What is Goth?* Newburyport, MA: Weiser Books, 2004.

Voltaire is an excellent writer, and this tongue-in-cheek look at gothiness is a fine example of his craft, as well as being an informative and interesting read. The author is clearly an insider, and his book is written in such a way as to provide a fun read for outsiders and an amusing diversion for fellow goths who do not mind making fun of themselves a bit. While the book is amusing, some of the essays and sections make strong arguments for a new way of looking at goths that contradicts the media's standard of fear and suspicion. Taken together, it is an informative and entertaining collection of goth trivia, tidbits, and musings.

Voltaire. *Paint It Black: A Guide to Gothic Homemaking.* Newburyport, MA: Weiser Books, 2005.

Voltaire's guide to the goth decorator is amusing and entertaining while simultaneously illustrating some of the facets that make goth culture unique and interesting. With an artistic eye, Voltaire discusses how to purchase goth-appropriate décor and how to transform "mundane" furnishings into darkly beautiful accoutrements. Though Voltaire's writing is often comical, he also has a clever way of displaying his love and affection for the culture he both lampoons and celebrates. Recommended for anyone interested in knowing what makes goths tick, or who might simply like the diversion of some more sinister surroundings.

Yoshinaga, Masayuki. *Gothic and Lolita.* London: Phaidon Press, 2007.

This is a photography compendium documenting the fashion of Japan's Gothic Lolita trend. Interesting photographs tell the story of how goth has spread around the world and now blends with elements of other cultures, including fetish and anime fashion. An excellent book for those interested in exploring the range of gothic fashion.

Film and Documentary

Finlay, Jeanie (writer, director), Natisha Dick (producer), and Nikki Parrot (producer). (2008). *Goth Cruise: The Movie* [Documentary]. United Kingdom: IFC & Tigerlily Productions.

Finlay's excellent documentary follows 150 goths traveling on a cruise ship from New Jersey to Bermuda. Though the concept sounds like the setup for a spoof, the subject is real and Finlay's coverage reveals many different aspects of the experience, from humor to horror. The film boasts a colorful cast of characters including writer/artist Voltaire, whose books are part of the basic canon of goth literature, and musician Andi Sexgang, singer and leader of the foundational goth band Sexgang Children. In addition to excellent production, the commentary from the documentary's subjects is intimate and revealing, helping to shed some light on who the goths are and what they do in nice weather.

Web Resources

Alt.gothic Official Site. "About Alt.gothic." 2008. http://www.altgothic.com/wiki/index.php/Alt.gothic.

> The official Web site for the alt.gothic community, this site provides information about the history of the newsgroup and its current function. Formed by a collective of volunteer users, the information on the site is interesting and informative and also demonstrates how the voluntary contribution of net.goths continues to keep the online community active. This site also provides information about the alt.gothic Convergence gathering, one of the largest goth gatherings in the United States.

Dark Grave. "Gothic Culture." 2009. http://www.darkgrave.com/articles/gothic-culture.php.

> Dark Grave is a Web site dedicated to goth music reviews and previews, but it also features a number of interesting articles about goth culture in general. One of the most interesting is the editor's rebuttal to information circulated through a Christian Web site accusing goth culture of promoting satanic behavior. In addition, Dark Grave provides an example of how those in the subculture treat and promote their own music. An interesting read for newcomers to the genre.

Gothic Beauty. "About Us." 2010. http://www.gothicbeauty.com/.

> *Gothic Beauty* is one of the most polished goth magazines available and has almost started to transition into the mainstream environment, now sold in many book and magazine outlets. The magazine features music and fashion reviews, centerfold displays, articles on a variety of subjects, and excellent photography. On their Web site, the folks at *Gothic Beauty* (started in 2000) provide lists of helpful links and a variety of sample articles and photographs.

Gothic.net: Bone Chilling Literary Culture. "Fiction." 2008. http://www.gothic.net/_blog/category/fiction/.

> Gothic.net fills a specific niche by providing information and resources related to goth literature, where most sites focus primarily on music. Gothic.net provides original stories as well as excerpts and links to goth

books, both classical and modern. In addition, the site invites user commentary and involvement through forums, attempting to create a community-style discussion group around the gothic literature fascination.

Goth Net. "Writings." 2002. http://www.goth.net/writings/index.html.

The Goth.net project pulls together a variety of gothy things under a single site, providing articles, music and fashion reviews, interviews, and even a healthy spattering of gothesque poetry. Though the site has fallen into relative obscurity, there is a healthy amount of information still available on the pages, providing an introduction to goth culture and in-depth views of subjects told from an insider's point of view.

Lenham, Tom. Goths in Hot Weather: A Celebration of the Sunshine Goth. 2010. http://www.gothsinhotweather.com/.

Goths in Hot Weather is a blog collecting photos of goths in sunny environments. After some time in production, the site began receiving hundreds of photos and videos sent in by goths themselves getting in on the joke. Lenham's photo blog pokes fun at the goths but also provides a variety of imagery showing goths around the world, though often not in their "natural" environment.

Lovely Corpse. "About." 2010. http://www.lovelycorpse.com/about.htm.

Gothesque artwork from Philadelphia-based artist Troy X. Musto. Musto blends classical influences with training in graphic illustration to create original artwork that is haunting, sensual, and elegant. Focusing primarily on the female form, Musto's art has a distinctive sense of the goth romanticism and provides an interesting example of a contemporary and highly imaginative take on the genre.

Mercer, Mick. "The Mick." 2009. http://www.mickmercer.com/.

Mercer is self-described as the longest running goth and punk music writer, and his work is known in goth circles worldwide. His Web page features access to his PDF format zine "The Mick," with reviews, commentary, and other articles written by the master of goth himself. Also featured on these pages are some of Mercer's past albums and information about all of his past and current book projects, each of which is an important contribution to goth culture and community.

Scathe, Pete. "An Early History of Goth." 2010. http://www.scathe.demon.co.uk/histgoth.htm.

This site provides a wealth of information on goth history and other fascinating parts of the pre-goth British landscape. Scathe is clearly intimately familiar with his subject but also conducts research worthy of a scholarly text on the subject. Scathe does not confine himself to goth alone, but wanders across seventies and eighties Britain, giving readers a taste of the history and passion that created punk, post-punk, and goth. Worth reading for beginners and those with a good handle on goth history.

Vamp. "The Goth Music Handbook." 2008. http://www.vamp.org/Gothic/Text/gothlist.html.

The editors at Vamp.org have created an interesting overview of some of the most influential and interesting goth bands out there, aiming for new audiences while also providing some gems that may have fallen under the radar of old fans. What Vamp lacks in production, it makes up for by being a very thoughtful collection of essential goth music ranging from the very old to modern iterations of the idea.

Index

45 Grave (band), 21, 94

Abbo. *See* Abbot, Steven

Abbot, Steven: biography, 82–84

Adams, Douglas, 101

Aesthetics: in art, 33; in goth fashion, 31, 39, 41, 108, 118, 124, 129; of goth music, 17, 18, 26, 29, 47 90, 92; of goth subculture, xi, xii, xiii, xiv, xv, 1–3, 7, 14, 28, 41, 44, 49, 59, 72–78, 83, 105, 106, 115, 116, 118, 120, 121

Album artwork, 19

Alt.gothic, 10–11, 62–64

Androgyny: in male goth fashion, 3, 26, 36–37, 92, 108, 120

Athey, Ron, 94–95

Authenticity, xv, 38–40, 67

Ayukawa, Norie, 39, 131

Ballion, Susan. *See* Sioux, Siouxsie

Batcave (club), 7, 120

Batman (film), 107

Bauhaus, 6, 20, 52–53, 83, 86, 91–93, 118, 120, 122, 137

Beetlejuice (film), 54, 106–7

"Bela Lugosi's Dead" (song), 6, 52, 91. *See also* Bauhaus; Murphy, Peter

Belgium, 24

Bellevue murders, 11

Bizarre Bazaar, 65

Black: in aesthetics, 32–34; significance in goth subculture, 6, 32–35, 38–41, 44, 72, 76, 77, 117, 128, 133

Black Tape for a Blue Girl (band), 21, 23, 27, 136, 137

Body modification, 34–35; contact lenses, 43; fangs, 35, 42, 43, 50, 64, 78; piercings, 34, 35, 71, 128–29; tattoos, 34, 71, 94, 128

Bowie, David, 3, 5, 20, 37, 52, 88, 89, 91–92, 93, 95, 118; biography, 84–87
Brennan, Sean, 23, 81. *See also* London After Midnight
Brind, Simon. *See* Count Von Sexbat
Brite, Melissa Ann. *See* Brite, Poppy Z.
Brite, Poppy Z., 50–51, 116; biography, 103–6
Bromley Contingent, 5, 96
Brooks, Joseph, 7
Burton, Tim, 53–55, 118–19; biography, 106–9

Cabinet of Dr. Caligari (film), 52
Christian Death (band), 7, 21–22, 26, 93–94, 137
Cities: Chicago, 27, 64, 137; London, 3, 4, 6, 7, 82, 83, 85, 91, 96, 124; Los Angeles, 8, 21, 23, 94–95, 118, 123, 137; New York, 4, 8, 27; Philadelphia, xv, 39, 42, 64; San Francisco, 64, 99
Clothing: and goth costume, 8, 26, 32–35, 37, 40, 43, 44, 108, 119, 125–26, 128–29; historical trends in, 38–39, 75; and punk, 5, 32–35; specialty vendors, 39, 61, 65; and subcultural significance, 35, 37–39, 69, 70
Columbine massacre, 12, 138
Community, 59–68; and the Internet, 11, 60–63; local and national, 23, 26, 40, 60; and music, 7, 23, 60–63; and the press, 59–62; translocal, xi, xv, 11, 12, 60
Conformity: in mainstream society, 56, 96; to subcultural standards, 35, 70
Constantine, Storm, 50–51
Convergence gathering, 64

Coon, Caroline, 5, 96
Counterculture, xiii–xiv
Count Von Sexbat, 62
Cure, The (band), 20–21, 75, 89, 97, 137
Curtis, Ian, 6; biography, 88–90
Cyberculture (goth), 10
Cybergoth, 9, 31, 38, 40–42

Dark Cabaret, 28, 138
Darkwave, 9, 64
Death: mythological character, 103; significance to the subculture, 32, 50, 72–73, 77, 100, 105, 116, 118;
Death rock, 8, 21–22, 38, 25, 93, 94
Depp, Johnny, 53, 107–8
Dir en Grey (band), 26, 123
Doors (band), 2–3
Dracula: book, 11, 48, 65; film, 42, 53, 53
Dracula's Ball, 11, 42, 64, 67

EBM (electro body movement), 9, 23–24, 29, 64, 138
Edward Scissorhands (film), 42, 53, 107–8
Ego Likeness (band), 64
Electronic music, 17, 23, 35, 41, 64, 77–78, 136
Elegant Gothic Aristocrat, 44
Elegant Gothic Lolita (EGL), 9, 26, 31, 43–44, 125–26
EMO, 63, 116, 121

Factory Records (label), 6, 116
Faith and the Muse (band), 23, 141
Fanzines, xiii, 7, 26, 61, 137
Fear Cult (band), 21, 123, 141
Fetish: in fashion, 9, 35, 42, 49, 64, 96, 129–30
Frankenstein: book, 48; film, 52

Gaiman, Neil, 49; biography, 101–3
Germany, goths in, xv, 10, 11,
    23–25, 32, 65–67
Glam rock, 3, 5, 37, 84, 86, 88, 91,
    94, 118, 120, 138
Goth gatherings, 11, 17, 42, 59, 62,
    64–67, 77, 128
Goth girl, 55, 102
Gothic architecture, 1, 6, 47–48
Gothic canon, 72
Gothic fiction, 1, 42, 44, 50–53,
    55–56, 72, 98, 99, 100, 104–5,
    119, 120, 142, 143–44
Gothic horror. *See* Gothic fiction
Gothic literature. *See* Gothic fiction
Goth nights, 7, 9, 17
Goths (Germanic tribe), 1
Great Old Ones, 62

Harajuku Street, 26, 44, 125–26
Homophobia, 70
Homosexuality: in gothic fiction, 50,
    51, 105; in goth subculture, 37
Horror: in film, 51–53, 55, 118;
    in goth culture, 12; in goth
    fashion, 31, 39, 44; literature, 1,
    42, 47, 48, 49, 103–6, 132, 141
Hot Topic, 8, 40, 119
Hunger, The (film), 52,
    86, 92
Hyde's Vice, 39, 131, 133–35

Iggy Pop, 4, 88
Industrial metal, 9, 19, 22
Internet: and cultural expansion, 11;
    and goth community, 59, 61–64,
    78, 120; and music distribution,
    27, 28, 138
Interview with a Vampire: book, 49,
    99; film, 42, 53, 100
In the Flat Field (album), 91

Japan, 25, 26, 32, 43, 44, 125–26
Joy Division (band), 6, 20, 21, 60, 75,
    88–90, 117

Karloff, Boris, 51, 52

Lacuna Coil (band), 74
London After Midnight (band), 23,
    81, 118
Lost Souls (book), 50, 104, 106,
Lovely Corpse, 75
Love Spirals Downwards (band),
    27, 137
Lugosi, Bela, 51–53
Lycia, 27 (band), 64, 137

Magazines: fanzines, xiii, 7, 26, 61,
    137; fashion, 123, 124, 125–29,
    131; music, 4, 5, 7, 10, 23, 60, 82,
    84, 86, 96, 123, 131, 135, 139
Mail order: fashion, 61, 131; music,
    26, 27, 61, 131, 136, 137
Malice Mizer (band), 26
Manson, Marilyn, 22
Matrix, 83
McLaren, Malcolm, 4
Media: negative portrayals of goths,
    xii, 11–12, 18, 109; role in goth
    culture, 7, 59, 123, 135–36.
    See also Magazines
Medieval rock, 24, 66
Melody Maker (magazine), 5, 60,
    86, 96
M'era Luna, 11, 66, 67,
Mercer, Mick, 7, 10, 60, 62, 63
Moi Dix Moi (band), 26, 44
Murphy, Peter, 52; biography, 91–93
Musto, Troy X., 75

Neo folk, 10, 25, 65; definition
    of, 113

Neo-medieval music, 24

Net goths (net.goths), 61, 63–64; definition of, 113

New Grave (magazine), 123, 125, 126, 131, 132, 133, 140. *See also* Riser, Matt

New Music Express (magazine), xix, 6, 89

New Orleans, LA, 64, 99, 104–5

New wave (music), xviii, 4–5, 20–21, 24, 29, 34, 89

New York Dolls (band), xviii, 4, 93

Nightmare before Christmas, The (film), 53, 108

Nine Inch Nails (band), 9, 22

Nosferatu (film), 52–53, 83

O'Brien, Howard Allen. *See* Rice, Anne

Oh My Goth (book), 49. *See also* Voltaire

Painter, Roger Alan. *See* Williams, Rozz

Panache (magazine), xix, 7. *See also* Mercer, Mick

Peel, John. *See* Peel Sessions

Peel Sessions, xviii, 4, 89

Plastic Records (label), 83

Pneumania (band), 83

Poe, Edgar Allan, 72, 77–78, 118, 141–42

Post punk: environment, 7, 18, 77; music, 2, 4–5, 7, 20, 88, 91, 111

Pratchet, Terry, 102

Price, Vincent, 108

Projekt (label), 8, 27, 136–39

Psychedelic rock, xvii, 2, 61

Punk: music, xvii–xviii, xix, 2–5, 18, 20, 26, 60, 82–84, 88–90, 93, 95–97, 115, 118, 120; fashion, 4,

34, 36, 43, 69, 83; subculture, 4–7, 19, 60–61, 91, 94, 117, 119. *See also* Glam rock; Post punk; Steampunk

Racism, 51, 70

Ramones, The (band), xviii, 4

Rapture (album), 97. *See also* Cure, The

Ravenscroft, John. *See* Peel, John

Recruitment, 13, 76

Reed, Lou, 3, 95. *See also* Velvet Underground

Remiet, Pierre, 76–77

Reznor, Trent, 9

Ricci, Christina, 108

Rice, Anne, xix, 42, 49, 53, 104, 120 (*see also Interview with a Vampire*); biography, 99–100

Riser, Matt, 123–25. *See also New Grave*

Rodgers, Patrick, 64. *See also* Dracula's Ball

Rosenthal, Sam, 27–29, 136; interview with, 136–39. *See also* Projekt

Ryder, Winona, 54, 106

S&M: in fashion, 9, 38; in the subculture, xx

Sandman (comic), xx, 49, 101

San Francisco, CA, 64, 99

Saville, Peter, 6

Scientology, 101

Scott, Tony, 52, 86. *See also Hunger, The*

Scream (album), 96. *See also* Sioux, Siouxie

Seraphim Gothique (band), 64

Sexism, 37, 70

Sex Pistols (band), xviii, 4–6, 88, 96, 122

Sexuality: in goth culture, 9, 25, 35, 70, 86, 120, 130; in gothic fiction, 50–51, 98, 100, 102, 104–6

Sexual preference, 37–38, 86, 102, 120, 130

Shadow Project (band), 22, 93–94. *See also* Williams, Rozz

Shelley, Mary, xvii, 48, 106. *See also Frankenstein*

Sioux, Siouxsie, xviii–xix, 5–6, 9, 20, 38, 118, 120, 137; biography 95–97

Sisters of Mercy (band), xix, 21, 140

Slimelight (club), xx, 7

Small Wonder (label), 91

Smith, Robert, 20, 97, 127. *See also* Cure, The

Social networking, xv, 9, 13, 27–28, 59, 61–62, 64, 115, 118

Sociology: of goth culture 18, 37–38, 71, 115; subculture research, xiv, 36, 40, 117

Sounds (magazine), xix, 60, 82–83

Spon, Steven 83. *See also* Abbo

Stardust, Ziggy, 38, 86–87, 91. *See also* Bowie, David

Steampunk, 41–42, 116; definition of, 113

Stoker, Bram, xvii, 11, 42, 48, 52, 65

Stooges (band), xviii, 4

Subcultural capital, 18, 24, 32, 66

Subcultures: absorption into mainstream, xiv–xv, 40; life cycle, xi, xiv, 12, 13, 17, 28, 40, 48, 74–76, 78; study of, xii–xiii, xiv, 5, 13, 35–36, 56, 59, 62, 69–71; types of, xiii, 1, 31, 42

Sunshine Blind (band), 64

Switchblade Symphony (band), 64

Symbolism: Celtic, 71; Christian, 34, 36, 52, 75, 100, 119; Druidic, 71

Teenage violence, xii, 11–12, 138

T-Rex (band), 21, 91, 93

True Blood (television series), 48

Uk.people.gothic, 63

Unknown Pleasures (album), xix, 6, 89

Usenet goths. *See* Net goths (net goths)

Vampire: clothing, 9, 19, 31, 50, 64, 72, 76, 92; definition of, 113; films, 42, 52–53, 78, 83, 86, 92, 98, 119–20; fiction, xix, 11, 48–50, 65, 98–100, 104, 119–20, 141, 143–46; goth, 31, 35, 42–43, 65

Veil (club), xix, 7

Velvet Underground (band), 2–3, 88

Victorian Cult of Mourning, 39

Vijuaru kei. *See* Visual kei

Visual kei, xxi, 25–26, 43–44, 65, 123, 125; definition of, 113

Voltaire (band), 27, 49, 137, 150–51

Walpole, Horace, 48

Warner, Brian Hugh. *See* Manson, Marilyn

Wave-Gotik-Treffen, xx, xxi, 65

Whitby Gothic Weekend, 11, 65, 128, 148

Williams, Rozz, 138 (*see also* Shadow Project); biography, 93–95

Wilson, Tony, 89

X JAPAN, 26, 126

Zig Zag (magazine), xviii, xx, 4, 7, 60

About the Author

MICAH L. ISSITT is a freelance writer living and working in Philadelphia. Issitt has a background in animal behavior research and has been writing professionally since 1999, contributing articles to newspapers, magazines, and academic publications. Since 2005, Issitt has been researching and writing about marginalized subgroups in human culture. Issitt is also the author of *Hippies* (Greenwood, 2009).